A MINISTRY SHAPED BY MISSION

A MINISTRY SHAPED BY MISSION

Paul Avis

t&t clark

Published by T&T Clark International

A Continuum imprint

The Tower Building   15 East 26th Street
11 York Road   Suite 1703,
London SE1 7NX   New York, NY 10010

www.tandtclark.com

British Library Cataloguing-in-Publication Data

A catalogue record for this book is available from the British Library

ISBN 0 567 08368 3 (Paperback)

Typeset by BookEns Ltd, Royston, Herts.
Printed on acid-free paper in Great Britain by Antony Rowe, Chippenham, Wilts.

CONTENTS

PREFACE

My hope for this book is that it will re-energize clergy, pastors and other ministers, ordained and lay, by clarifying and focusing their calling. I want all Christians who read it to gain a sense of where the ministry fits in God's good purposes for the world and what its key tasks are. The special contribution of this book, among the many modern studies of ministry, is to show what the ministry is *for* by integrating it with what the Church is *for*. If we can begin to answer the question, Why the Church?, we can then begin to answer the question, Why the ministry? And when we have reached some clarity about that, we can go on to tackle the further question, Why ordination?

I ought to make clear straight away perhaps what this book does and does not attempt. To put this briefly first of all:

- This book is not purely about 'the priesthood', presbyteral ministry, but is much wider than that vital ministry, setting out the theological grounding for all ordained and lay ministry.
- It is not a confessional account. Although written by an Anglican, it is not addressed only to Anglicans; its principles are quarried from ecumenical sources and its conclusions have ecumenical relevance.
- It is not specifically about the ordination of women to the priesthood and the episcopate, though my arguments indirectly support that development.
- It is not a comprehensive theology of ministry and ordination. This book is more sharply focused than that: it explores the pivotal connection between ministry and mission.

- It is not an abstract and timeless theological exposition (was there ever any such thing?), but is impelled by the urgency of our missionary situation in the West, in a culture that is increasingly being torn away from its Christian moorings by powerful secular and non-Christian currents.

Let me elaborate these points as a way of leading more deeply into the purpose and content of the book.

First of all, unlike some titles of this genre, this book is not simply about the ordained priesthood (or presbyterate), though it deals with it. The book is equally about the ministry of those who are, so to speak, not ordained ('lay people'), and about the ministry of deacons and bishops. But it is prompted by a sense that answers are needed to some fundamental questions about the meaning of ordination. I recognize, however, that those questions cannot be answered until we become clear about the meaning of ministry as such, which is a concept broader than ordained ministry.

Second, this book is not particularly addressed to Anglicans and is not directly about Church of England matters. Nevertheless, it seems to me to be relevant to both the Church of England and the wider Anglican Communion. A Communion and a Church that has been struggling to make up its mind about a whole raft of major ministry issues – women priests and bishops, the ordination of openly practising homosexual clergy and bishops, lay eucharistic presidency, 'local ministry', the distinctive diaconate, sequential ordination (deacon-priest-bishop) and 'extended communion' – certainly needs a robust theology of ministry and ordination.

Third, this book is not actually about the ordination of women. I have written about aspects of that issue before (Avis 1989, 1999a) and I have recently edited a collection of studies on the 'reception' of this development and the condition of 'being in communion' that is needed to enable the process of reception/discernment to occur (Avis, ed. 2003b). However, what I say towards the end of this book about the significance of ordination to our understanding of the diaconate and its relation to the mission of the whole people of God is highly relevant to the issue of women's ordination. Anglicans generally opposed to the ordination of women made little fuss about women's ordination to the diaconate: to my mind that step is theologically crucial, in terms of holy order, sacramental ordination, as the Roman Catholic Church seems to recognize.

Some years after women were first ordained to the priesthood in the Church of England, a bishop, who was himself opposed to the ordination of women, told me that he had interviewed all the women priests for whom he was responsible. He found that they seemed to have a very hazy idea of what ordination to the priesthood was all about. I would not go so far as to say that he took a grim satisfaction in this finding – I hold him in better esteem than that – but I suspect that it confirmed him in his view. I felt obliged to point out, however, that, if he had put the male clergy through their paces in the same way, the result might have been similar. The vagueness of ordinands about the meaning of ordination – a vagueness deplored by many involved in ministry matters – stems from the church culture from which they come before our training institutions get their hands on them, not from their sex. Some ordinands from a lively evangelical background are suspicious of anything that seems to set them apart from 'the priesthood of all believers': they sometimes say that they 'just want to serve the Lord full-time'. Some from a Catholic background (Roman or Anglican) are still trying to operate an unreconstructed clericalist model of ministry – 'by the few for the many', rather than the holistic paradigm advocated in this book, which we might call 'by the many for the whole' (cf. Weil 2002: 51; Greenwood 1994). But the shortage of a decent theology of ministry and ordination, to resource the training that ordinands receive both before and after ordination, no doubt plays its part. In turn, that training may be hampered by an unwillingness on the part of students to access what there is.

Fourth, I make no apology for the fact that this book does not attempt to deal with the whole range of issues concerning ministry and ordination (that would be a daunting task). Rather it explores the connection between the ministry of the Church and the mission of God and so brings out at a profound level the ultimate raison d'être of ministry and ordination. I am convinced that we will never understand the Church's ministry unless we first understand its mission within the mission of God (*missio dei*). My approach presupposes that we should begin from the nature and purpose of the Church. If we try to start straight away with questions about ordination or ministry, we are forced into a step by step regress until we reach bedrock and there gain a vision of the *missio dei*. Then we can begin to move forwards more confidently.

The greatest of twentieth-century missiologists, David Bosch, summed up a lifetime of reflection on mission when he wrote in *Transforming Mission* that mission 'is the good news of God's love, incarnated in the witness of a community, for the sake of the world' (Bosch 1991: 519). As Bosch implies in this pregnant definition, a full and comprehensive theology of mission needs to hold together three dimensions. The first is the content of mission: the character of the God who sends and the meaning of the gospel of God's redeeming love. The second is the instrument of mission: the nature and purpose of the Church that bears witness to that message and of its ministry and sacraments (the theological discipline of ecclesiology). And the third is the scope of mission: the world that is the object of God's love, and in particular the diverse and changing character of our culture and the place and role of the Christian faith within it.

The headline definition of mission suggested by Bosch sets an agenda for missiology, the scholarly study, or science, of mission. It implies that missiology needs to deal with three areas of theological understanding: the content, instrument and scope of mission. The first two areas of reflection, content (God and the gospel) and instrument (the Church and its ministry), ground missiology in biblical revelation and the tradition of Christian doctrine. The third area of study, scope (the world and its cultures), is vital to ensure that any programme for mission is not theoretical but is 'on target' – that is to say, thought through in the light of the social and cultural situation in which mission is conducted. That leads me to the next and final caveat.

This book is definitely intended as a theology of ministry and ordination for our times. It is suited to our condition and situation as Christians who are feeling increasingly pushed to the margins in our society (not so much in the United States, where Christian faith and churchgoing are still respectable and sometimes prestigious) and who are experiencing hostility from the culture-shaping media. In assessing whether Britain is still 'a Christian country' (as Voas does in Avis, ed. 2003a), we should distinguish between three arenas or spheres: first, the constitutional and legal structure of the state (not to be confused with the political party or regime that happens to be in power at any given time); second, the constellation of institutions that make up civil society; and third, the prevailing culture, including the mass media. In the United Kingdom, while the constitution of the state remains clearly Christian and the structure of civil society still makes room for the role of the Churches, contemporary culture is not supportive, but rather subversive of the Church and of Christian beliefs. Where culture leads, civil society will almost certainly follow and eventually the constitution of the state will fall into line (cf. Avis 2001). Although I would be the first to point to the goodwill in very many parishes toward the parish church and what it stands for and to appeal to the upsurge of interest in spirituality that, sensitively handled, can create pastoral opportunities for the Church, I would not take anything for granted.

On the contrary, I would urge that the Church needs to be structured for mission and geared up for evangelization. *A Church Drawing Near: Spirituality and Mission in a Post-Christian Culture* (Avis 2003) is my attempt to relate mission to our elusive cultural context and to show how the pastoral ministry can be flexible and creative in negotiating that culture. That book is an applied theology and explicitly presupposes the theology of a ministry shaped for mission that is attempted here. In a recent volume of studies, *Public Faith? The State of Religious Belief and Practice in Britain* (Avis, ed. 2003a), a distinguished line-up of scholars in the social sciences and theology take us beneath the surface of the statistics that are sometimes bandied about in the media. They put us in touch with the rather inchoate spiritual aspirations and religious beliefs in our culture that are still infused with Christian symbols and meanings. Direct study of these contextual, cultural issues is not our purpose here. Our focus will be on the mission of God and the ministry of the Church. Together they comprise our theme: the mission of God that shapes our ministry.

Needless to say, putting it in this way – God's mission, our ministry – is not meant to imply that while the mission is God's, the ministry is ours. As we shall see very clearly in Part 2, all ministry is the ministry of God in Jesus Christ. It is neither our invention nor our possession. It is not at our disposal to do what we like with it, nor may we take the credit when it is successful. To state our theme as the mission of God that shapes our ministry is intended to lay the emphasis very firmly on the gracious sovereign initiative of God in relation to the world that God has made and to evoke a theological vision of the God who never ceases to pour God's love and goodness and grace into the world. It puts down a theological benchmark, whereby the ministry of the Church is placed unmistakeably in the wake of God's mission and is construed as a response to what God is already doing all around us, to what God has already done throughout history and will do in the future to accomplish God's infinitely loving and gracious purpose for the creation.

As so often, Hans Küng hit the nail right on the head in his book, published more than thirty years ago: *Why Priests?* (Küng 1972). In the churches some people are asking, why do we need priests when we have to pay for them ourselves? Why do we need clergy when they sometimes dreadfully let us down? Indeed, we might ask, why do we need ordained ministers when parishioners can write to *The Times* proudly claiming that they conduct their own family services and have little need of the clergy – 'and none of us is trained'? Why do we need priests when a theology class of mostly Christian, churchgoing undergraduates could tell me that they could not see the reason for an ordained ministry? Why, once again, do we need priests when some writers eloquently advocate lay celebration of the Eucharist (e.g. Marriage 1995)?

There is a theological challenge here – the gauntlet has been well and truly thrown down – as well as a pastoral and practical one. One acute practical issue is the shortage of candidates, especially young candidates, of suitable calibre for ordination, that many Churches are experiencing, some almost catastrophically. A chronic pastoral issue is the scandalous wastage of clergy and ministers who drop out because they are disillusioned or burnt out, or have to give up their ministry because they have fallen short of the required standard of personal behaviour. I am not under any illusion that these two – perhaps related – phenomena are patent of a simple explanation, or that a theological account of ministry that places it in the dynamic of the mission of God provides any kind of panacea for the strains and stresses of ministry today. But I am convinced that we need to pick up the challenge posed by Hans Küng in the ear-to-the-ground, tuned-in-to-Western-culture way at which he excels. And I am equally convinced that candidates for ordination, those involved in their selection, clergy and ministers who may very well be under stress and wondering about their calling, and lay people working on behalf of the Church in ministry would welcome answers to Küng's question, broadly interpreted, thus:

- What is 'ministry' and what is not?
- What is the biblical, especially New Testament, basis of ministry?
- Do all Christians have a ministry?
- Does the language of 'ministry' work any more?
- Why does the Church ordain some ministers but not others?
- Are deacons simply apprentice priests/presbyters?
- Why are bishops somehow special?
- Does God really care about all this?
- How does the Church's ministry connect with God's saving purpose for the world?

Some recent wise and useful writing on ministry, though often theologically articulate and pastorally helpful, does not go to the root of the problem posed by Küng on behalf of many genuine questioners today (particularly helpful exceptions to this failure include Greenwood 1994; Hall and Hannaford, eds 1996; Goergen and Garrido, eds 2000; Wood 2000; Wood, ed. 2003). The answer that I develop here begins from the insight that, in the Church, the mission of God takes the form of a ministry. I go on to expound this as a triple ministry of word, sacrament and pastoral responsibility, reflecting the Church's commissioning by Christ. I argue that it is not merely an historical accident that this ministry is ordered in the threefold form of bishops, priests and deacons, but that this structure of holy order is an ecclesial sign of the christological nature, pneumatological anointing and missionary purpose of the Church. Finally, I reconstruct this order, in the light of fresh biblical interpretation and of the urgency of mission and evangelism as that of deacons, priests/presbyters and bishops (that order, though also reversible on good grounds, is intentional here) and of lay people who also fully share in the mission of God and the ministry of the Church, being fundamentally ordered to that mission-ministry in their baptism and confirmation, just as the ordained are.

The argument of this book progresses through three stages.

- In the first main section we look at the *missio dei* that shapes the mission of the Church and see that the mission that is entrusted to the Church takes the form of a triple ministry of word, sacrament and pastoral responsibility.
- In the second part we examine the ministry that is shaped by mission and respond to the urgent need to clarify what actually qualifies as ministry and what is not properly ministry but straightforward Christian discipleship. We take our cue from the truth that all ministry is that of Christ in his Church, the Christ who is anointed Prophet, Priest and King. We allow fresh research into the New Testament's use of *diakonia* to shape our understanding of the missionary thrust of the ordained ministry.
- In the third and final part we consider how the whole Church is ordered in ministry and ask what ordination means and why some ministries are ordained and others not. We attempt to hold together two fundamental affirmations that are often polarized: the royal priesthood of the baptized and the sacramental understanding of ordination. We ask what difference ordination makes and what reforms and developments are called for in the Churches' understanding of ministry.

Professor Robert Hannaford's far-reaching essays 'Towards a Theology of the Diaconate' (Hannaford 1991) and 'Foundations for an Ecclesiology of Ministry' (in Hall and Hannaford, eds 1996) first prompted me to work on the idea of ordained ministry as an ecclesial sign and in that connection to scrutinize the prevailing functional understanding of *diakonia* as humble service (as soon as I began to do so, it fell right apart!).

I have adapted some brief material from my article 'From *Episkope* to Episcopacy' that appeared in *One in Christ* (36.3, 2000, pp. 223–33). Some of the ground was covered at a conference on the meaning of ordination that I convened under the auspices of the Centre for the Study of the Christian Church in Exeter in September 2003. I also presented some condensed material at the Second Theological Conference between the British and Irish Anglican Churches and the Nordic and Baltic Lutheran Churches under the Porvoo Agreement in September 2004.

I am deeply indebted to Professor Bruce Marshall, the Revd Professor Geoffrey Wainwright and the Revd Canon Professor J. Robert Wright for providing me with some incisive comments on a draft text as well as generous encouragement about the usefulness of the project. I thank Joanna Cox for some insights from the point of view of lay ministry.

Finally, I need to point out that I am writing in a personal capacity and not necessarily representing the views of the General Synod or of the Council for Christian Unity.

PAUL AVIS
Council for Christian Unity;
Centre for the Study of the Christian Church

THE MISSION OF GOD THAT SHAPES OUR MINISTRY

The totality of mission

How can we express the theological idea of mission in all its range and depth? There have been many studies of mission, but its nature has perhaps never been more exhaustively or helpfully examined than by David Bosch (Bosch 1991). I have already flagged up, as a sort of motto for this book, his statement that mission 'is the good news of God's love, incarnated in the witness of a community, for the sake of the world' (p. 519). For me to propose yet another definition may seem superfluous, if not arrogant, but it may help to bring our topic into focus. Adapting the well-known suggestions of others, I offer the following working definition of the mission of the Church: *Mission is the whole Church bringing the whole Christ to the whole world*.

In this holistic concept of mission, mission is seen as the cutting edge of the total life of the Church. That life is made up of many activities: prayer, worship, confession of faith, teaching and preaching, celebrating the sacraments, especially baptism and the Eucharist, providing pastoral care and oversight, enjoying Christian fellowship, bearing one another's burdens, bringing prophetic critique to bear on unjust social structures, and communicating the love of Christ to the suffering through compassionate service. If we say that mission is the cutting edge, so to speak, of the life of the Church as a totality, it follows that there is a Godward as well as a 'humanward' orientation to mission. Prayer, praise, the celebration of the Eucharist and the confession of the faith all have a primary orientation to God. Truly, the purpose of the Church is (as the Westminster Catechism classically put it) 'to glorify God and enjoy him for ever'.

In this study we are, however, immediately concerned with the orientation of the Church's purpose to the world and to humankind, especially to the non-Christian and the unchurched. But this aspect of mission will be fruitless and futile unless it is grounded in worship, prayer and the grace of the sacraments: from those activities it draws its life and power. This total concept of mission also ensures that we register the vital role of the sacraments in mission, especially in the process and pattern (*ordo*) of Christian initiation – indeed, that we have a sacramental, as well as a proclamatory concept of mission. A holistic missiology enables us to say that 'the entire missionary life of the Church is a true and living sacrament of the universal salvation in Jesus Christ' (Osborne 1988: 286).

Now let us look at our working definition more closely. Mission is the task entrusted to *the whole Church*. The Church is an apostolic or missionary body. To confess at the Eucharist, in the Nicene-Constantinopolitan Creed, that the Church is apostolic is to confess that it is a missionary Church: the two terms are simply the Greek (*apostello*) and Latin (*mitto*) forms of the verb 'to send'. Just as Jesus Christ was sent into the world on behalf of the Father, he sends the Church into the world on his own behalf. And just as all that Jesus said and did was motivated by his overpowering consciousness of being sent, so all that the Church does and says should be so motivated (John 20.21b; cf. Matthew 10.40; Luke 10.16; Kruse 1983: ch. 3).

If it is true, as I shall argue shortly, that the mission of the Church in the world takes the form of a ministry, we must say that not only mission but ministry also is entrusted to the whole Church, not just to the ordained. Every baptized believer is potentially (though I shall argue, not automatically) a minister. The Catechism or Outline of the Faith in the Book of Common Prayer of the Episcopal

Church of the USA asks: 'Who are the ministers of the Church?'. The right answer – and the only answer that is possible if the Church is a missionary body – is: 'The ministers of the Church are lay persons, bishops, priests and deacons.' An evangelical church in Westminster, London, has on its notice board: 'Pastor: The Revd So-and-So'; 'Ministers: The Congregation'.

In mission the whole Church brings *the whole Christ* to the whole world. If, as Augustine said, 'the whole Christ is the head and the members', he is already present in and with his Church in its mission, just as he had promised to be: 'I am with you always, to the end of the age' (Matthew 28.20). The Church does not *import* Jesus Christ into a situation, for he precedes every action of the Church and does not need the Church's permission to be present. Neither does it *transport* him into places where he was not present already, for he is present, at work and found by many in every place and time, through the universal Spirit of God. So Christ is not dependent on the Church, on its mission and ministry. Perhaps it is not appropriate to say that the Church 'brings' him. The initiative is his: if anything, he brings the Church, carrying it forward in the momentum of his mission. However, he has chosen to work through the Church and bound himself to her by his promises, especially the Great Commission (Matthew 28.18–20), by the gift of his Spirit (Luke 24.46–48; John 20.22–23; Acts 2.1–4) and by the sacraments of salvation, baptism and the Eucharist, the dominically appointed means of grace. In the celebration of the sacraments the minister does what the Church does and does it in the name of Christ and in obedience to his command. In the sacramental action the whole Church is acting. The authentic ministerial actions of the Church are catholic, universal actions of the whole Church. So the whole Christ is revealed and received in his word and his sacraments where these are ministered in the spirit of compassionate care shown by the Good Shepherd (Luke 15.3–7; John 10.1–18).

In mission the whole Church brings the whole Christ to *the whole world*. This is not simply a geographical denominator, though the universal scope of mission is certainly not in question. The emphasis falls on wholeness. The world is full of persons. The gospel is not preached to stocks and stones, nor to flocks and herds, nor to the birds and the bees. They are by no means outside of God's care and our human responsibility, but they are not 'hearers and doers of the word' (James 1.22–25; cf. Romans 10.17). It is persons, created in the image of the personal God, who are on the receiving end of mission. Its goals, values and methods must be appropriate to their personhood and not ride roughshod over it. In mission, people are sent to people: mission takes place person to person, face to face. Where that personal and relational dimension is compromised, mission is compromised: it becomes distant, mechanical, unreal and ineffective. In mission, the Church draws near to individuals, households, families and communities in the name of the Person of Jesus Christ. It seeks to lead them into greater wholeness by drawing them, through the extended process of Christian initiation, into the life of the Christian community as the Body of Christ. It ministers among them and to them in the personal mode, in a relational framework. Ministry is not primarily a set of functions, but a self-giving of one's whole person, imperfect and in need of being made whole as it is. We approach the world as ourselves part of the world, but a part that has been touched by Christ already (for this pastoral approach to mission see Avis 2003).

The mission of God

Nothing less than this holistic definition of mission is called for because our whole life as Christians – our entire Christian existence in this world – is inherently geared to mission. Christian existence is orientated to the loving purpose for the world that flows from God's plan of salvation. Here we are speaking of the theological axiom of the universal salvific will of God that is revealed in Jesus Christ. The Second Vatican Council (1962–65), in laying down the doctrinal principles of the missionary activity of the Church, affirmed that 'the pilgrim Church is missionary by her very nature' (Abbott, ed. 1966: 585 [*Ad gentes* 2]).

Underlying the teaching of Vatican II here is the profound concept of twentieth-century ecumenical theology, that of *missio dei*. The Latin term is necessary because it holds a depth and power that English translation cannot capture: the mission of God, the mission that belongs to God, the mission that flows from the heart of God. *Missio dei* speaks of the overflowing of the love of God's being and nature into God's purposeful activity in the world. As the Council put it: 'Freely creating us out of his surpassing and merciful kindness, and graciously calling us, moreover, to communicate in life and glory with himself, he has generously poured out his divine goodness and does not cease to do so' (Abbott, ed. 1966: 585 [*Ad gentes* 2]).

The concept, if not the precise language, of *missio dei* originated in Protestant theology with Karl Barth in the early 1930s. In a way that was typical of Barth's theological emphasis, he began to speak of mission as an activity, not of human beings, but of God. The idea, though again not the term, first surfaced explicitly at the Willingen conference of the International Missionary Council in 1952. The statement of this conference said:

> The missionary movement of which we are a part has its source in the Triune God himself. Out of the depths of his love for us, the Father has sent forth his own beloved Son to reconcile all things to himself ... We who have been chosen in Christ ... are committed to full participation in his redeeming mission. There is no participation in Christ without participation in his mission to the world. That by which the Church receives its existence is that by which it is also given its world-mission. (See special issue of *International Review of Mission*, 92, no. 367 (2003), at p. 464)

In the theological movement signalled by Willingen, mission was seen to derive from the very nature of God and was interpreted in the light of the Church's confession of faith in the Holy Trinity. According to this insight, Father, Son and Holy Spirit together send the Church into the world in mission. Christian mission is an expression of the movement of God towards the world: the Church is an instrument of this movement. Mission precedes Church. The Church exists because God's mission – in the profound, nuanced sense of *missio dei* – is under way. As Bosch puts it: 'The *missio dei* is God's activity, which embraces both the Church and the world, and in which the Church may be privileged to participate.' Therefore, Bosch concludes, we can say that 'mission has its origin in the heart of God' (Bosch 1991: 391; cf. 389ff).

The insight that stems from both Protestant and Roman Catholic sources, concerning the *missio dei*, has been extensively received and appropriated in the various Christian traditions and now belongs to the mainstream ecumenical consensus. For example, the report of the Dialogue on Mission between Evangelicals and Roman Catholics, that ran from 1977 to 1984, states: 'Mission arises from the self-giving life and love of the triune God himself and from his eternal purpose for the whole creation' (Gros *et al.*, eds 2000: 409).

Because mission is the overflowing of God's love in order to reconcile the world to God, it has an eternal and cosmic dimension. *Missio dei* encompasses and enfolds the world and the Church. It reflects the prevenient (going before) grace of God. Mission is much bigger than the Church. It is not restricted to the Church. It does not depend, in any final sense, on the Church. Christian mission is fundamentally a response to the initiative of grace that has already brought the Church into being. Moltmann describes the *missio dei* as 'a movement from God in which the Church has its origin and arrives at its own movement, but which goes beyond the Church, finding its own goal in the consummation of all creation in God' (Moltmann 1977: 11).

The prevenient reality of *missio dei* means that Christians are not in the futile business of attempting to bring an absent Christ to an abandoned world. God is already ahead of us in mission. We are following in the footsteps of the Lord, discovering where he is already at work and through whom he is working (Sugden in Samuel and Sugden, eds 1999: 232). Mission is premised on the theological conviction that Christ is already present to the world through the continual universal operation of the Holy Spirit. When a parish priest with a special ministry to prostitutes in London's East End was asked recently whether he managed to talk to them about God, he replied, 'No, they talk to *me* about God.' The biblical witness is emphatic that God is at work in mission in innumerable ways – not only in individual lives and the life of families, but in communities, in civil society and in the history of nations.

Mission belongs to God and is filled with God's reality. But its primary content is Jesus Christ and the gospel. Its vital power is the power of the Holy Spirit. And its primary instrument is the Church. Vatican II said of the Church: 'it is from the mission of the Son and the mission of the Holy Spirit that she takes her origin, in accordance with the decree of God the Father' (Abbott, ed. 1966: 585 [*Ad gentes* 2]). So we may legitimately extrapolate from the language of *missio dei* and speak also of *missio Christi, missio spiritu sancti* and even, though in a firmly secondary and derivative way, of *missio ecclesiae*.

The New Testament tells how God purposed in Christ to reconcile and unite the world to himself (Ephesians 1.10; Colossians 1.20). God was uniquely present in Christ to accomplish this (2 Corinthians 5.18). God invites unworthy but redeemed human beings into partnership in God's mission, making them ministers of reconciliation (2 Corinthians 5.18). In mission the Church seeks to do nothing more – and nothing less – than to reflect and proclaim the person and work of Christ. In doing this it is reflecting and proclaiming what lies at its very heart. For it is Jesus Christ who constitutes the very life of the Church. His saving mission in the world has brought the Church into being and constituted it as the dedicated instrument of his ongoing mission. That is why mission belongs to the essence of the Church. 'The Church lives by mission as a fire lives by burning.' The Church participates in the reconciliation that Christ has accomplished. It exists as a fellowship of reconciliation in itself and is sent into a divided and alienated world with a message of reconciliation. 'The Church must proclaim the reconciliation by which it lives and live out the reconciliation it proclaims' (Torrance 1966: 141).

Evangelicals and Roman Catholics were agreed, in the Dialogue on Mission (1977–84), that 'the church continues and prolongs the very same mission of Christ' (Gros *et al.*, eds 2000: 426). In the New Testament there is a *missiological identity* between Christ and the Church. In John the risen Christ imparts his power and his authority to the Apostles with the words, 'As the Father has sent me, so I send you' (John 20.19–23). In the Great Commission at the end of Matthew, Jesus sends the Apostles to make disciples of all nations and promises to be present with them even to the end of the age (Matthew 28.18–20). Luke makes it clear that repentance and forgiveness are to be proclaimed by the Church to all the nations 'in his name' (Luke 24.47). The book of Acts presents the Apostles as Christ's witnesses in the power of the same Spirit that rested upon him (Acts 1.8). Murray Dempster points out that 'Luke-Acts makes it clear that the mission and ministry of the Church is to replicate the mission and ministry of Jesus through the power of the Holy Spirit' (Dempster in Samuel and Sugden, eds 1999: 51). But this is in fact true of the New Testament material in its entirety. As Alan Richardson put it: 'The ministry of the

Church is the continuation of the apostolic and priestly ministry of Christ himself ... his ministry to the world is fulfilled through the instrumentality of his resurrection body, the Church' (Richardson 1958: 291).

The mission of the one Church

If mission can be described as the cutting edge of the total life of the Church, it is integrally related to the Church's corporate existence as the Body of Christ. This means that mission and unity can never be separated: they are twin attributes of the Church as God has created it and intends it to be. The 'theological logic' of this connection is worth exploring.

As the Second Vatican Council affirms, God's loving purpose for the humankind that God has created cannot be achieved in a purely individualistic or private way but only corporately and publicly. The *missio dei* works (though not exclusively) through the community or society of people brought into being by God, namely the Church, the new Israel. The Council broadly presupposes here the theological anthropology (theology of human nature) developed by Karl Rahner SJ (d. 1984). Rahner stressed the truth that human existence cannot be understood simply as the existence of individuals. It is not atomistic, but is inherently structured by our collective social life. It is not episodic, it does not just pop up here and there, but is embedded in the continuities and discontinuities of history. Rahner's emphasis needs to be heard and heeded more than ever in today's postmodernistic fragmentation of community and radical privatization of values.

As the instrument of salvation, the Church reflects the character of human existence and of the redemption that God has provided in Christ. So the Church, too, is socially and historically structured and could not fulfil its mission unless it were so constituted. This structured community, the Vatican Council teaches, has been endowed with the means of grace, principally word and sacrament, to bring about the participation of humankind in the transforming life that flows from God. The purpose for which the Church exists is to bring to bear on the life of individuals and communities the salvific (saving) means of grace ordained and provided by God.

> The mission of the Church, therefore, is fulfilled by that activity which makes her fully present to men and nations ... Thus, by the example of her life and by her preaching, by the sacraments and other means of grace, she can lead them to the faith, the freedom and the peace of Christ. (Abbott, ed. 1966: 589f. [*Ad gentes* 5])

In his major teaching on evangelization in the modern world (*Evangelii nuntiandi* 1975), Pope Paul VI insisted that evangelization is primarily an 'ecclesial' not an individual task: the whole Church evangelizes (Flannery, ed. 1982: 740f.). Because the content of mission is Jesus Christ and the gospel, it is inherently ecclesiological, not a piece of private enterprise. It is the Church as the Body of Christ that is the agent of mission. This body exists in several forms: as the local worshipping community or parish, as the diocese in which the bishop is the chief pastor, as a national or regional Church (as Anglicans particularly would say), and also, though outwardly fragmented, universally. Mission is entrusted to the whole Church as a structured society with ordered means of grace. As the task of the Church, mission is the vocation and responsibility of all baptized believers, the *laos*, the redeemed and sanctified 'people of his own' (Titus 2.14; cf. 1 Peter 2.9), without distinction, at this point, between ordained and 'lay'. The Church, with all the means of grace that bring salvation, aims to be 'fully present' (as Vatican II put it) to communities, culture and society through the presence of lay and ordained Christians to every part of society.

Because mission is an action of the Church, it is an ecclesiological matter. This means that the unity of the

Church is inevitably a dimension of mission. The profound biblical connection between mission and unity has been affirmed by the ecumenical movement since its inception, certainly since the Edinburgh Missionary Conference of 1910. Recent ecumenical texts bind unity and mission closely together. In this they are reflecting an ecumenical consensus that draws on the theological vitality of the Second Vatican Council. Although the Council's teaching contains strong hierarchical and juridical elements, inherited from centuries of centralization and control, it is also marked by a strand of organic, integrated, holistic ecclesiology in which mission and unity are indissolubly connected. Vatican II portrays the Church's outreach to needy humanity as her participation in the overflowing grace and love of God that is being constantly poured out for the salvation of the world. The mission of the Church is grounded in the mission of the Father, the Son and the Holy Spirit.

The Dogmatic Constitution on the Church begins on a note of evangelical fervour:

> Christ is the light of all nations. Hence this most sacred Synod, which has been gathered in the Holy Spirit, desires to shed on all men that radiance of his which brightens the countenance of the Church. This it will do by proclaiming the gospel to every creature (cf. Mk. 16.15). (*Lumen gentium* I, 1)

It immediately shows that this mission cannot be achieved without unity: 'By her relationship with Christ, the Church is a kind of sacrament or sign of intimate union with God, and of the unity of all mankind. She is also an instrument for the achievement of such union and unity' (ibid.).

The Decree on Ecumenism of Vatican II (*Unitatis redintegratio*) strikes what is today an unfashionably anti-individualistic note. It has no time for consumer preference where the gospel is concerned. It does not suggest that people might 'shop around' for the most attractive Christian package. It begins by acknowledging that disunity damages mission. 'The Church established by Christ the Lord is, indeed, one and unique.' Yet there are many Churches and many voices. 'Without doubt, this discord openly contradicts the will of Christ, provides a stumbling block to the world, and inflicts damage on the most holy cause of proclaiming the good news to every creature' (*Unitatis redintegratio*, I, 1).

When the Council comes to speak of mission in the decree *Ad gentes*, it locates this in the fundamental divine commissioning and constitution of the Church: 'The pilgrim Church is missionary by her very nature. For it is from the mission of the Son and the mission of the Holy Spirit that she takes her origin, in accordance with the decree of God the Father' (*Ad gentes*, I, 2).

But the Church's unity is equally fundamental. God did not send the Church merely to address individual human beings in their private interiority, but as humankind, in their collective, social nature. The Church rightly calls people into a community, one that is ordered by structures, sustained by sacraments and overseen by pastors. 'Missionary activity wells up from the Church's innermost nature and spreads abroad her saving faith. It perfects her catholic unity by expanding it' (*Ad gentes*, I, 6). In this way, the decree continues, echoing biblical language, God's purpose to gather into one his human creation is realized: 'According to this plan, the whole human race is to form one people of God, coalesce into the one body of Christ, and be built up into one temple of the Holy Spirit' (*Ad gentes*, I, 7).

Partly through the ecumenical reception of the Second Vatican Council and partly as a result of other influences, especially the theology of Karl Barth, an integrated, holistic ecumenical theology developed. *God's Reign and Our Unity* (1984), the report of the international Anglican-Reformed dialogue, is a striking example of an ecumenical dialogue that sets the quest for visible unity in the context of the missionary nature of the Church. 'Mission is the sovereign action of the Holy Spirit' and 'the work of gathering all the nations to become God's people and to worship him from whom their life comes, is the work of God himself' (GROU 38). The report expresses the conviction that this perspective puts differences between the churches in a fresh light (GROU 35–38).

The Anglican-Lutheran *Niagara Report* (1988) succeeded in tackling difficult questions of church order and ministry in the light of a theology of the gifts that God has given to his Church to resource mission. Its approach bore fruit in the Porvoo Common Statement, published under the title *Together in Mission and Ministry* (1993). In these texts, the method of beginning with the *missio dei* enabled a breakthrough to be made on issues of ministry.

As an example of the integration of mission and unity in recent ecumenical dialogue, we may take two or three documents involving Anglicans and Methodists. The report of the informal conversations between the Church of England and the Methodist Church of Great Britain, *Commitment to Mission and Unity*, argued that 'the Gospel message of communion with God, with one another and with the world is compromised by our divisions, and consequently our witness to reconciliation is undermined.' The Church's own life should exhibit the unity and peace which God intends for the whole of creation. (*Commitment to Mission and Unity*, para. 43).

The report of the Anglican–Methodist International Commission *Sharing in the Apostolic Communion* shows that there is a reciprocal relationship between mission and unity; they promote each other: 'We acknowledge that mission is both empowered by God's gift of unity within the Church and implements and makes visible the Church's unity for the world to see and believe' (Anglican–Methodist International Commission 1996: para. 37).

The British Methodist Conference statement on ecclesiology, *Called to Love and Praise* (1999), links mission and unity by grounding them both in the triune nature of God: 'The unity of the Church and its mission are closely related, since the Triune God who commissions the Church is One, seeking to reconcile and bring the world itself into a unity in Christ' (*Called to Love and Praise*, 1999: para. 3.2.1).

Finally, the report of the Formal Conversations between the Methodist Church of Great Britain and the Church of England, *An Anglican–Methodist Covenant* (2001), takes the integration of mission and unity as its guiding thread and contains a substantial exposition of this theme. Clearly neither Anglicans nor Methodists are interested in coming closer together unless that is grounded in a commitment to united mission, shared witness and the visible expression of 'the unity of the Spirit in the bond of peace' (Ephesians 4.3).

The mission of the one God must become the mission of the one Church and its integrity and effectiveness are compromised until it is!

Mission and evangelization

If mission is the cutting edge of the whole life of the Church, it cannot be reduced to evangelization or evangelism (I use the Protestant form 'evangelism' and the Roman Catholic form 'evangelization' interchangeably and without trying to make a point). Mission and evangelization cannot be identified because mission is bigger than evangelization. Evangelization is a *part* of which mission is the *whole*. As Moltmann puts it: 'Mission embraces all activities that serve to liberate man from his slavery in the presence of the coming God, slavery which extends from economic necessity to Godforsakenness. Evangelisation is mission, but mission is not merely evangelisation' (Moltmann 1977: 10). Evangelization is mission focused and directed in a particular way. Bosch defines evangelism as 'the proclamation of salvation in Christ to those who do not believe in him, calling them to repentance and conversion, announcing forgiveness of sin, and inviting them to become living members of Christ's earthly community and to begin a life of service to others in the power of the Holy Spirit' (Bosch 1991: 10f.).

New Testament terms can help us to distinguish between evangelism and mission. In the New Testament evangelism takes three closely related forms.

- First, evangelism is to tell good news (*evangelizesthai*): we might say that this is its joyful annunciatory aspect.
- Second, it is to bear witness (*marturein*): this is its testatory aspect, the giving of solemn testimony.
- Third, it is to proclaim a message (*kerussein*): this is its fearless proclamatory aspect.

From this brief analysis it appears that evangelism is a dynamic activity. It is energetic, outgoing and aims to make an impact. It is largely verbal in character and consists of the communication of meaningful statements (propositions). Altogether, evangelism as the New Testament understands it could be described as essentially 'kerygmatic' or proclamatory (Green 1970: 48ff.).

If, on the other hand, we wanted to get a picture of the New Testament idea of mission, as distinct from evangelism simply, we would need to add several substantives to these verbs.

- The first would be *leiturgia* (communal worship or liturgy, offered to God; literally, 'the work of the people').
- The second would be *diakonia* (commissioned work in the service of God).
- The third would be *koinonia* (fellowship or communion between Christians in the Church and between the Christian community and God the Holy Trinity).

This further brief analysis suggests that mission is a broader notion than evangelism. Mission involves as much action as articulation. It has an essential liturgical – and I think we must say, sacramental – dimension. The idea of mission can embrace the entire life of the Church in a way that the concept of evangelism cannot.

In 1987, the then Board of Mission and Unity of the Church of England came up with 'Ten Marks of Mission'. These ranged from the sound but predictable ('To witness to the good news of Jesus and the Kingdom'), through the thought-provoking ('To advance in the discernment of God in company with others'), to the prophetic ('To identify and challenge the corruption of power'). The BMU compared mission to a cut diamond 'of which no single facet can display its beauty and complexity' ([Board of Mission and Unity] 1987).

A few years later, the Anglican Communion was offered a more economical list, 'The Five Marks of Mission', by the Anglican Consultative Council ([Anglican Consultative Council] 1990: 101f.) and these were endorsed by the Church of England's General Synod in 1996. Evangelism comes first, but is set in a wider context:

- to proclaim the Good News of the Kingdom
- to teach, baptize and nurture new believers
- to respond to human need by loving service
- to seek to transform the unjust structures of society
- to strive to safeguard the integrity of creation and sustain and renew the life of the earth.

This summary has proved serviceable in many arenas of Church and inter-Church life. But we can see at a glance that it is deficient. Although it has a broad sweep and does not take mission as equivalent to evangelism – the latter being only one of five activities – there is no mention of worship offered to God and particularly of the Eucharist as the centre and summit of worship. If mission is about the God-given purpose of the Church, what the Church is called to be, what it is for, then all the essential tasks of the Church must be included. Mission is the driving force of the total life of the Christian Church.

Clearly mission is a rich and multifaceted reality. It includes a wider range of operations than evangelism. What must be at least implicit in all dimensions of mission – God's offer of eternal salvation through Jesus Christ – is necessarily explicit in evangelism. In *Evangelii nuntiandi* Pope Paul VI affirmed:

> Evangelisation will always contain, as the foundation, the centre and the apex of its whole dynamic power, this explicit declaration: in Jesus Christ who became man, died and rose again from the dead salvation is offered to every man as the gift of the grace and mercy of God himself. (Flannery, ed. 1982: 722)

Yes, the content of the evangelistic message will be profoundly Christological. As Paul VI splendidly says: 'There is no true evangelisation if the name, the teaching, the life, the promises, the kingdom and the mystery of Jesus of Nazareth, the Son of God, are not proclaimed' (ibid.: 720).

It is significant that immediately after each of the two World Wars, with all their death, suffering and misery, the Church of England addressed the urgency of evangelism and reflected on what it entailed. In 1918 The Archbishops' Committee of Inquiry on the Evangelistic Work of the Church produced this magnificent, though rather dated definition:

> To evangelise is so to present Christ Jesus in the power of the Holy Spirit, that men shall come to put their trust in God through him, to accept him as their Saviour, and serve him as their King in the fellowship of his Church.

The later report *Towards the Conversion of England*, published at the end of the Second World War, endorsed this robust statement of the scope and purpose of evangelism (Church Assembly 1945: 1).

Between these two Church of England reports came a classic ecumenical statement. *The World Mission of the Church* was the published report of the 1938 Tambaran conference of the International Missionary Council. As the dark clouds of global war gathered, especially in Europe and the Far East, the conference spoke of 'The Unfinished Evangelistic Task'. The commission to preach the gospel to every creature was given to the Church universal in all its branches and to all its members. The Tambaran conference memorably defined evangelism as 'to so present Christ Jesus to the world in the power of the Holy Spirit that men shall come to put their trust in God through him, accept him as their Saviour and serve him as their Lord in the fellowship of the Church' (*The World Mission of the Church*: 33).

The Tambaran conference also soundly emphasized the ecclesial nature of evangelism. 'World evangelism is the God-given task of the Church.' It is inherent in the nature of the Church as the Body of Christ, created by God to continue the work of Christ, to evangelize. Tambaran by no means overlooks the missionary challenge of social transformation and the imperative to work for justice, freedom and peace. But the dominant theme is the Church's calling 'so to exalt and proclaim' Jesus Christ that people are won to repentance, faith and participation in the Church (*The World Mission of the Church*: 33–42).

An holistic understanding of mission not only affirms the priority of evangelization but relates it to the life of the Church. Tambaran affirmed that the purpose of evangelism is nothing less than to incorporate new Christians into the life-giving milieu of the Body of Christ. As William Abraham says, evangelism is 'governed by the goal of initiating people into the kingdom of God' (Abraham 1989: 95). It is, therefore, a polymorphous activity, involving the whole range of the means of grace and providing a viable foundation for Christian nurture. One activity on its own (such as preaching) is not sufficient to constitute evangelization. Evangelization flows from the life of the Church and returns to the life of the Church. It cannot be conceived of without the structured provision of word, sacrament and pastoral care. As Abraham insists, one cannot enter the kingdom while being outside the Church, for it is through baptism, in the context of faith, that a person sacramentally enters the Israel of God, 'that body where God reigns supreme in worship and praise' (p. 130).

The life of God that indwells the Church and in which we participate by faith and the means of grace, principally word and sacrament, is the communion (*koinonia*) constituted as an objective reality by the abiding presence of the Holy Spirit in the Church. The Christian mystery is made present and effective through the tasks for which the Church has been commissioned. That mystery is supremely expressed in the enactment of worship, culminating in the celebration of the Eucharist – for in worship the power of imagination, of beauty and form, of sound and sight is evoked to glorify God. Corporate worship creates, challenges and reinforces the imaginative picture we treasure of God and God's purposes, a picture that shapes our faith and life. As Neville Clark puts it: 'The celebration of baptism and Eucharist, the proclamation of preaching, the range of worshipping response, will alike image in uncounted ways the reality of Jesus Christ and will communicate configurations of him' (Clark 1992: 59). In a similar vein, the Orthodox Consultation on 'Confessing Christ through the Liturgical Life of the Church Today' states: 'Proclamation should not be taken only in the narrow sense of an informative preaching of the Truth but above all of incorporating man into the mystical union with God' (Abraham 1989: 60).

There is, however, a depth and fullness in mission that evangelization alone cannot attain. As an expression of *missio dei*, the Church's mission conveys God's saving power in its fullness and wholeness for the healing of humanity (cf. Titus 2.11). True mission considers humankind, not as a collection of souls, disembodied spiritual essences, but as an embodied social, cultural and historical reality. That is precisely why, as I have argued in *A Church Drawing Near* (Avis 2003), belonging comes before believing for most people. A sense of attachment, however unarticulated, to the community of faith and a consciousness, however inchoate, of having a stake in all that it stands for and has stood for over the centuries is a prerequisite for a living faith. The fact – so troublesome for world evangelization – that very few people change the religion in which they have been brought up for another testifies to the inextricable link between believing and belonging. But that is how we are made. The will of God for the wholeness and healing of human life can only be realized in social, communal terms. It requires Christians and Churches to work for greater social, political and economic justice and well-being, as well as to proclaim the gospel in word and sacrament.

Evangelization brings into sharper focus what the Church stands for at all times and in all its activities and is therefore an essential component of mission. As Archbishop George Carey stated: 'Mission which does not have evangelism as a focus is not Christian mission; and evangelism which keeps itself aloof from matters of justice and human welfare does not reflect adequately the biblical revelation' (Carey 1997: 7). Mission and evangelization are thus integrally related and grounded in the same biblical, theological principle: that the Church carries out its God-given task by doing the things that it has been commissioned to do. Mission, and within it evangelization, is the Church being the Church and living out the totality of its life, grounded in grace. What precisely is this commission? My contention – to be expanded in what follows – is that *the Church is commissioned to carry out a ministry of word, sacrament and pastoral care.*

I doubt whether many Christians would question the claim that the ministry of the word, the administration of the sacraments and the provision of pastoral care are central to the Church's purpose. But I imagine that some would challenge my contention that they comprise the mission of the

Church exclusively and without remainder. So let me explain. I am not attempting to put mission in a straitjacket. I have no wish to place artificial limits on the diversity of forms that mission takes. I fully acknowledge, as proper and vital aspects of Christian mission in its broadest sense, such areas as social action, religious and moral education, political activity in the cause of justice and peace, and the nurturing of personal wholeness through many forms of therapy. They are activities that are infused with the Christian gospel and carried out in the service of Christ. I do maintain, however, that to justify themselves in terms of the Church's mandate these activities should relate at some point – and the more closely they relate the better – to the ministry of the word, the sacraments and pastoral care since these are the God-given, the divinely ordained, tasks of the Church.

The tasks of the Church

At a meeting of a diocesan synod the speaker was waxing eloquent about the Church's calling to minister the word of God, celebrate the sacraments and provide pastoral care in the parishes of the land. When the speaker had finished, the first comment from the floor asked, in effect: 'That's all very fine, but haven't you forgotten something? What about the *mission* of the Church?' It is a common misconception that mission is a separate, discrete function of the Church, an activity in which it engages over and above its basic, bread-and-butter tasks. It is often assumed that this triple ministry (word, sacraments, pastoral care) takes place independently of the Church's mission, as though mission were something added to the continuous, ordinary life of the body of Christ, rather than the outworking, the leading edge of its very existence. The biblical *locus classicus* of missiology, the 'Great Commission', suggests a rather different perspective.

In Matthew 28.19–20 the triple ministry of word, sacrament and pastoral care is implied: 'Go therefore and

21

make disciples of all nations, baptizing them in the name of the Father and of the Son and of the Holy Spirit, and teaching them to obey all that I have commanded you.' The authenticity of this text, as a saying of the historical Jesus, is generally discounted. But in order to take this text as a fundamental charter of Christian mission, we do not need to assume that the words are the *ipsissima verba* of Jesus, that they fell from his lips in that form. It seems unlikely that Peter and Paul's preaching to the Gentiles would have aroused intense opposition (Acts 10–12, etc.) if there had been an explicit command of Christ to the Apostles to make Gentile disciples. On the other hand, however, nothing less than Christ's personal authority would have been needed to enable the first Christians to break out of the strongly Jewish confines of the early community and its mission (Gundry 1994: 596). This consideration, combined with the broadly parallel texts to the Great Commission in Luke 24.44–53, John 20.21 and Acts 1.8, points to the essential authenticity of the Great Commission, in the sense that it is true to Jesus's intention for the post-Pentecost, apostolic Church.

However, there is a further difficulty in appealing to the Great Commission as the basis of the Church's mandate. It is difficult to deny the argument that it is implausible that the precise form of the Trinitarian baptismal formula can be traced back to the immediately post-resurrection period. It is found only here and in the *Didache* in the first century and probably reflects later baptismal practice. On balance, then, the most that we can claim for the Great Commission is that it embodies Christ's intention for his Church. At any rate, it has canonical authority as authentic apostolic teaching and I propose to take it on the strength of that. (For a thorough discussion of these issues see Le Grys 1998, especially pp. 40–51.)

In the Great Commission we read of three activities that Jesus commanded: making disciples, teaching, and baptizing.

Jesus had already shown the way, modelling all three tasks. He had called Peter and Andrew, James and John, the fishermen and Matthew the tax collector, as well as other members of the Twelve, to follow him (Matthew 4.18–22; 9.9; 10.1–4). Now the whole world is to be called to discipleship. To be a disciple is, literally, to be a learner in the school of Christ the Teacher. Matthew emphasizes the teaching ministry of Jesus. He introduces the Sermon on the Mount with considerable formality and deliberation: 'When Jesus saw the crowds, he went up the mountain; and after he sat down, his disciples came to him. Then he began to speak, and taught them, saying ...' (Matthew 5.1–2). Jesus identifies himself as their one Teacher or rabbi (Matthew 23.8). He combines teaching, both in the open air and in the synagogues, with preaching or proclaiming the gospel and healing the sick (Matthew 9.35). Having already been exhorted to teach all the commands of Christ (Matthew 5.19), the disciples are later sent out to proclaim the gospel and to heal the sick (Matthew 10.7–8).

They are not, however, instructed to baptize. Among the four gospels, only John (4.1–2) mentions that the disciples baptized on behalf of Jesus. However, the fact that the Apostles insisted from the beginning of the post-Pentecost mission that baptism was essential to discipleship and to salvation (Acts 2.38) is readily explicable if they had practised baptism during Jesus's own ministry. But in all four gospels Jesus passes through baptism himself at the hands of John the Baptist and it is Matthew who emphasizes that he does this in strict obedience to the will of God and therefore he receives the divine seal of approval, the descent of the Spirit (Matthew 3.13–17). To follow Jesus through the waters of baptism is the appointed way of initiation into the community of disciples who keep Jesus's word.

In the Great Commission each specific activity that is commanded by Jesus stands for a particular wider area of the Church's ministry. Teaching equates to the ministry of

Discipling?
pastoral ministry?

the word; baptism to the ministry of the sacraments and making disciples to the ministry of pastoral care and oversight. As Pope John Paul II says, in this text 'the entire pastoral ministry can be seen as organized according to the threefold function of teaching, sanctifying and governing' (John Paul II 2003: 7).

As a later section of this book will expound in greater depth, the triple task of ministering word, sacrament and pastoral care corresponds to the threefold messianic office of Jesus Christ. He has a threefold anointing, being empowered by God as Prophet, Priest and King. The triple task also corresponds to the threefold vocation of ordained ministers to teach, to sanctify and to govern (shepherd or lead) the Church. The laity must also play its part in this threefold calling since they also participate by baptism in the threefold messianic identity of Jesus Christ (as Vatican II makes clear: Abbott 1966: 26–30 [*Lumen gentium* 10–12]; Osborne 1988: 307–42).

I have argued that mission is not a separate, discrete activity of the Church, over and above everything else that it does in its everyday life. Let us apply this text to a classical Reformation text. The Church of England's Thirty-Nine Articles of Religion (1571) describe 'the visible Church of Christ' as a community of Christians ('a congregation of faithful men') in which the pure word of God is preached and the sacraments are administered according to Christ's ordinance (Article XIX). Here the Articles are echoing the Lutheran Augsburg Confession and a broad Reformation consensus about what is defining of the Church and how it can be known. It is easy to leap to the conclusion that here the Articles have overlooked the need for mission, since only word and sacrament are mentioned.

Now it is fair to say that the Articles presuppose a Christian society in which there is no one who is not within the congregation or *ekklesia*. (Jews and Muslims were the two non-Christian groups best known to the sixteenth-century Reformers, but neither were part of English society in the sixteenth century – the Jews, having been expelled from England in 1290, were not readmitted until Oliver Cromwell's regime in the mid-seventeenth century.) The Articles presuppose that Church and State are two aspects of the one unified community. Christian and citizen are two roles of the same person. There was little sense, in this context, of 'outreach', of moving out to those who were beyond the sphere of faith. There was nobody out there: they were all within the fold. However, given that caveat, the Articles cannot be dismissed or patronized. There is a deep wisdom in this Article – the wisdom that the Church carries out its mission precisely by preaching the word and administering the sacraments. These are the tasks of the Church; they are what it is here for.

Thus the Porvoo agreement of 1993 between the British and Irish Anglican Churches and the Nordic and Baltic Lutheran Churches states: 'We believe that the Church is constituted and sustained by the Triune God through God's saving action in word and sacraments' (Porvoo 1993: para. 32(f); broadly following Meissen 1992: para. 16(vii)). However, the ministry of word and sacrament do not exhaust the tasks of the Church; they do not exclusively comprise its mission. A ministry of word and sacrament that was not set in the context of pastoral care and oversight would be impersonal and mechanical – it would not have that relational, person-to-person, face-to-face quality that we earlier identified as the key to effective mission and for that reason alone it would be missiologically disastrous. So Porvoo adds: 'We believe that a ministry of pastoral oversight (*episcope*), exercised in personal, collegial and communal ways, is necessary as witness to and safeguard of the unity and apostolicity of the Church' (Porvoo 1993: para. 32(k); following Meissen 1992: para. 15(x)).

Now let us look more closely at the three primary tasks of the Church that comprise its mission.

The word in mission

Let us begin here with the Christian tradition that probably most typically affirms the centrality of the word – the tradition of the Reformation. According to the consensus of Reformation theology, the Church is identified by the twin actions of preaching the word of God and rightly administering the sacraments (as Article XIX of the Thirty-Nine Articles implies). The Reformers believed that the preaching of the gospel creatively brought the Church into being, for in this dynamic way Christ was active in the world for our salvation. For Luther, it has been well said, 'only the proclamation of the word is necessary to create the Church ... The Church is nothing else than the miracle of the power of the word appearing in a new form' (Althaus 1966: 290; cf. Avis 1981: ch. 1). There is no question that the power and centrality of the word is determinative of the Protestant tradition. But it would be a mistake to set this over against modern Roman Catholic theology, as though that also did not strongly affirm the creative power of the word.

Vatican II states (echoing Mark 1.14–15; 16.20) that Jesus Christ inaugurated the Christian Church by preaching the gospel and that the Apostles gathered together the universal Church by the same means (Abbott, ed. 1966: 17, 39 [*Lumen gentium* 5;19]). In *Evangelii nuntiandi* Pope Paul VI affirmed that the saying ascribed by Luke to Jesus, 'I must preach the good news of the kingdom of God', 'sums up in a word the whole mission and mandate of Jesus'. The unfolding of his destiny – the drama of salvation history – is determined by this announcement. Paul VI also insisted in this encyclical that there should be 'the closest link, ... an unbroken connection, between the word and the sacraments' and that they should never be ministered separately (Flannery, ed. 1982: 713f., 731). A wholehearted emphasis on the word is not the exclusive prerogative of the Reformation tradition, but is true of the whole Christian Church in its manifold forms.

The ministry of the word takes two forms, proclamation and teaching. It comprises proclaiming the gospel by every possible appropriate means and expounding the Scriptures to provide instruction in the faith. To preach the gospel of Christ, which is the power of God for salvation (Romans 1.16), is a primary task of the Church. But along with proclamation (*kerygma*) goes instruction (*didache*) whereby the faithful are built up as the body of Christ (Ephesians 4.12). Both these tasks of the Church are essential to its mission because they are expressions of its apostolicity. For the Church is apostolic when it is not only grounded in the apostolic proclamation but also faithful to the Apostles' teaching (Acts 2.42). Faithfulness to the essential characteristics of the apostolic Church of the New Testament is what makes the Church of today apostolic in its mission (BEM 1982: M34).

However, the ministry of the word, whether in the form of proclaiming the gospel or in the form of teaching the faith (catechesis), is not a monologue, a unilateral activity. It is not that one party speaks and the other party listens. For the word to be received there must be a genuine conversation, leading to a meeting of minds. Today more than ever, the Church's ministry of the word must take the form of a dialogue. As Pope Paul VI insisted in his first encyclical *Ecclesiam suam*, the Church must listen as it speaks and it must respond to what it hears. Both listening and response should be marked by pastoral sensitivity, empathy and respect. If this is the posture that the Church as a whole should adopt, it should filter through to every particular concrete instance of preaching and teaching. The spoken or unspoken questions that arise in this context are: Does this make sense to you? What does your own experience tell you about that? Can you agree with this? What would help you to receive what the Church is saying? Where do the stumbling blocks lie? How would you put it yourself? The ministry of the word as conversation, as dialogue, as heart-to-heart, not as take-it-or-leave-it, is akin to Paul Tillich's 'method of correlation' between human questions and revealed answers, in which there is a continual mutual interaction, negotiation and communication between the two. What is quite clear and incontrovertible is that today there can be no communication without conversation. That is not to allow distorted and potentially idolatrous human imaginations to shape the word of God. The sovereignty and transcendence of the word remains. It is simply to ensure that communication takes place. Only in this way can the ministry of the word serve the cause of mission.

The sacraments in mission

Celebrating the sacraments instituted by Jesus Christ belongs to the tasks of the Church alongside the ministry of the word. The performance of the sacraments has two foci. The first and most immediate focus is obviously the worship offered by the Church. To offer to God adoration, thanksgiving and intercession belongs unquestionably to the mission entrusted to the Church. But this cannot be separated from the second focus, that of the world to which the Church, bearing word and sacrament, is sent. The primary motive for evangelism is 'God's love for the world eliciting our praise' and that, therefore, 'a praising community is an agent of evangelism' (Sykes 1995: 203–6).

The second focus of the sacraments is, then, the public world and its needs. The celebration of the sacraments is not the private ritual of an in-group. It is not the Church talking to itself. It is a primary act of witness and of evangelism. The act of baptizing is a visible point of impact in the world. Although the activities of teaching and pastoring (or making disciples) obviously have visible elements, not least the people concerned themselves, baptism is a visible, meaningful sign. 'Every baptism service is intended to be in the eye of the world at large, and not simply for the benefit of the congregation and the candidate. It is the witness, not simply of the candidate ..., but of the whole Church to the whole world' (Ritchie 1967: 40).

The Eucharist, too, is a public demonstration of Christ's death and resurrection. 'For as often as you eat this bread and drink the cup, you proclaim the Lord's death until he comes' (1 Corinthians 11.26). The Greek suggests: 'You are continually proclaiming or showing.' The verb *kataggello* is used routinely in the New Testament to mean announcing or proclaiming the gospel (1 Corinthians 9.14), preaching the word of God (Acts 13.5), or preaching Christ (Acts 4.2; Philippians 1.17–18). It carries overtones of a public declaration that is effective, performing a declarative speech-act openly (Thiselton 2000: 886–7). Neither baptism nor the Eucharist can be celebrated in secret, in camera, without losing something vital to their purpose. Ideally they should be at the centre of public attention.

These two foci of sacramental celebration – the Church's worship and the public world – should not be polarized. The sacramental principle holds them together. The sacramental spirituality of the Catholic tradition (including, of course, Anglicanism) refuses to divorce worship from the workaday world. It is theologically predisposed to find the grace of God at work in the 'natural' structures of the world and of society. It aspires to forge links between the liturgical life of the Church and the values of the communities with which the Church interacts. It is just such an incarnational, embodied, sacramental understanding of the gospel that informs our present exposition of the mission of the Church. For the sacraments – together, needless to say, with the word – are the very life of the Church and constitutive of its divine–human identity. 'For Christians the sacraments are more than rituals. They are the Church itself, for the Christian Church is the common life of the persons, divine and human, who constitute it' (Grainger 1988: 77). The Christian life is nothing less than a sacramental continuum.

Together with baptism and the Eucharist we can include in this sacramental continuum various other expressions of the sacramental principle, of sacramentality, involved in worship: hymnody and choral liturgy, church architecture and decorations, liturgical vestments and even sacred dance. Wherever the word of God is joined to significant actions to comprise an outward visible sign of an inward spiritual grace the sacramental principle is at work. These physical signs are indispensable. As Louis Weil has written: 'Through their physicality the sacraments correspond to our physical nature, so that as the expression of love involves not just an interior attitude but the whole person, so is it also with faith: faith requires an enfleshing, a response in which the whole physical being is involved.' Quoting Tertullian's dictum 'The flesh is the hinge of salvation' Weil goes on, 'The outward, physical aspects of the sacraments are the instrumental means by which faith articulates both God's gift of grace and the human acceptance of the gift' (Weil in Sykes *et al.*, eds 1998: 78; cf. Weil 2002).

BAPTISM

Baptism is the fundamental sacrament of Christian initiation (though not 'complete sacramental initiation', as is sometimes alleged). That process of initiation is continued sacramentally in Confirmation, with its personal confession of faith and the strengthening of the Holy Spirit. It is completed in the sacrament of the Eucharist, when we offer ourselves, all unworthily, as a living sacrifice (Romans 12.1) in union with Christ's perfect oblation of himself on the cross, and receive his Body and Blood – the whole Christ – in Holy Communion. First Communion completes Christian sacramental initiation, the bringing about of which is the central task of evangelization. The Eucharist manifests and deepens our incorporation into the mystical Body of Christ and thus into the *koinonia* (communion, fellowship) of the Church.

Baptism consists of three elements: the sacramental action with the element of water (the 'matter' of the sacrament); the accompanying performative words ('I baptize you') with their Trinitarian formula (the 'form' of the sacrament); and the context of the faith and practice of the Church (the intention to do as the Church does). There can be no sacrament without the integral contribution of the word. The foundational sacrament of baptism is thus a ministry of word and sacrament. Christians are united in their baptism with Christ in his death and resurrection (Romans 6.3–11) and thereby brought into a covenantal union with him (Galatians 3.26–29).

With its symbolism of descent and ascent, death and resurrection, and new birth from the womb, baptism powerfully proclaims the mystery of salvation. For Jesus, baptism was his consecration to the work of human salvation. Its outworking led him forward to Gethsemane, Calvary and the garden of the resurrection. Through all the scenes of his earthly life and ministry, Jesus was a representative person, the corporate servant of the LORD, the Son of Man, the truly human one. He had pledged himself in solidarity to his people by joining in the baptism of repentance to which John the Baptist had summoned the whole nation. Baptism is not a series of repeated acts of ablution (*baptismoi*) but a great objective act of God (*baptisma*), received through the response of faith. 'The true baptism is then the great divine–human drama of redemption, from incarnation to glorification, in which God incorporated our humanity into his own divine life. The sacramental act of baptism is the vivid and effective symbol of our incorporation into that event, just as it was Jesus' vivid and effective inauguration of his destiny' (Avis 1990: 28). As T. F. Torrance has written: 'Christ's vicarious baptism was his whole living passion culminating in his death, his baptism in blood, once and for all accomplished on the cross' (Torrance 1959: II, 113). Or as

John Robinson put it: 'The baptism of Jesus is his whole existence in the form of a servant' (Robinson 1953: 259).

Baptism is one of the tasks given to the Church by its Lord as part of its mission (Matthew 28.19; cf. Mark 16.16). The Church should not be niggardly about baptism or offer it grudgingly: we are commanded to baptize all nations. Provided it is done in a theologically and pastorally responsible way, Christ wants his Church to baptize with all its might, in season and out of season. Because baptism is primarily not an expression of human response, but a mystery wrought by God in prevenient grace, it proclaims and shows forth the death and resurrection of Christ (just as the Eucharist does) and liberates his life-giving power. Baptism is, therefore, a vital instrument of evangelization.

THE EUCHARIST

The Eucharist sets forth the Christian mystery in its totality for our heartfelt assent and personal participation. In the Eucharist, including the Communion within it, Christians are more deeply and strongly united to one another and to Christ. He gives himself to his people in, with and under the forms of bread and wine and draws them into the movement of his self-offering to the Father (ARCIC 1982: Eucharist 5). The Church's work (*leiturgia*) in the sacrament of the Eucharist is broadly threefold.

- First, to offer thanksgiving (*eucharistia*) by rehearsing the mighty saving acts of the Triune God, culminating in the Incarnation, life, ministry, passion and resurrection and ascension of Jesus Christ and his sending of the Holy Spirit.
- Second, to make a dynamic memorial (*anamnesis*) of Christ's unique and complete self-offering to the Father and to make the cross of Christ our own in the sacramental action.

- Third, to receive once again the whole Christ in Communion and to be sent forth, in the assurance of his continuing presence, to be his witnesses in the world.

All three elements, severely condensed here, can be accomplished only by virtue of that union with Christ in his Body that has already been established by grace and given in the *koinonia* of baptism.

Like baptism, the Eucharist has the character of a public sign. In the New Testament sense, it is a *musterion*, a mystery that is manifest through revelation. It was not an arbitrary matter when the Greek *musterion* (e.g. 1 Corinthians 2.1; Ephesians 5.32) was translated into the Latin *sacramentum*. The nature of a sacrament, as an outward, visible sign of an inward spiritual grace, resonates with the biblical concept of mystery. The mystery that is Jesus Christ is not something ethereal and unworldly (though it is utterly sublime), but is an embodied fact in the world. We come up against it, engage with it, grapple with it – and it with us. Although the spiritual truth of the mystery, including the sacraments, is only fully apparent to the eyes of faith (1 Corinthians 1–2), it remains the case that the sacraments have always been primary indicators of Christian, ecclesial identity.

The Eucharist is, as David Ford points out, a multidimensional, extravagantly overdetermined sign. It preaches the gospel through action, drama and the semiotics of corporate event, as well as through the written and the spoken word. 'It is hard to overestimate the importance for Christianity of the fact that the eucharist, a pivotal locus of its identity, is a corporate practice, rather than, say, an ethical code, a worldview, a set of doctrines, an institutional constitution [or] a book ...' (Ford 1999: 140; cf. 137, 144–5). As we have already noted, St Paul is clear that the actions of eating the bread and drinking the wine proclaim, show forth or preach the death and resurrection of Christ (1 Corinthians 11.26).

Although the Eucharist (unlike baptism) is not mentioned in the Great Commission, celebrating the Eucharist was one of the tasks given from the beginning to the Church (1 Corinthians 11.24–25). The celebration of the Eucharist (like baptism) is a work that the Church is called to perform, not simply as the heart of its worship, but as an act of evangelization. Therefore, to bring about participation in the Eucharist is a primary goal of mission.

There is a dynamic connection between baptism, as the fundamental sacrament of initiation into the Body of Christ, and the Eucharist in which the reality of the Body of Christ is brought to light most clearly. Samuel Taylor Coleridge believed that baptism and Eucharist together comprised 'Christianity itself' (Coleridge 1884: 259–61). Christopher Cocksworth has claimed for the Eucharist 'a unique functional force and, thereby, a level of ontological intensity not ordinarily to be found in the other moments of Christ's activity in the Church' (Cocksworth 1993: 190). Quoting Louis Weil, he emphasizes that the Eucharist portrays 'in awesome simplicity' the essential features of the gospel (ibid.).

But does it make theological sense to elevate one dominical sacrament over the other? What Cocksworth claims of the Eucharist is surely no less true of baptism. Baptism, properly understood, also portrays in awesome simplicity the whole mystery of the gospel. It speaks of the solidarity of God with humankind in the Incarnation and unfolds the drama of death and resurrection. Baptism and Eucharist are complementary – and probably equally significant – modes of one divine redemptive action. Archbishop Thomas Cranmer wrote in his *Defence of the True and Catholic Doctrine of the Sacrament* (1550): 'Our Saviour Christ is both the first beginner of our spiritual life (who first begetteth us into God his Father), and also afterwards he is our only lively food and spiritual life.' Cranmer then discusses a passage from Hilary's *De Trinitate* where Hilary asserts that there is no difference between the Christian's union with Christ in baptism and in the Eucharist (cited by Sykes in Johnson, ed. 1990: 139–41).

Other expressions of the sacramentality of the Church's life are grounded in the essential ecclesial tasks of preaching and teaching the faith and celebrating the sacraments and therefore also comprise an integral part of the pastoral mission of the Church. Confirmation may be regarded as a pastoral application of the fundamental Christian initiation in baptism which, following further instruction in the faith and personal acceptance of it, is expressed in a sacramental way through the sign of the laying on of the hands of the bishop and prayer for the confirmation and strengthening of the Holy Spirit. Private confession and absolution (the sacrament of penance) may be requested by a penitent with a troubled conscience that is not assuaged by the general confession made in public worship. Here we have a further pastoral application of the gospel of salvation and of the one baptism for the remission of sins, a particular form of the ministry of word and sacrament. The Church's ministry of healing through the laying on of hands or anointing (James 5.14–15), enacted in faith and in the name of the Lord, is a further pastoral application of the ministry of the word added to the appropriate outward sign to a particular circumstance. The sanctifying of stages of life's journey in the occasional offices (the so-called rites of passage), such as marriage and funeral rites, are held within the framework of the ministry of word and sacrament and in the context of pastoral care (see further, Avis 2003).

Pastoral care in mission

The ministry of word and sacrament does not take place in a vacuum. It needs to be set in the context of effective pastoral responsibility to help Christians to put their faith into practice. Pastoral care provides support and guidance amid the dilemmas, temptations and afflictions of life. It fosters a personal application of Christian teaching to daily life. There is an emerging ecumenical consensus (reflected, for example, in *Baptism, Eucharist and Ministry* [BEM] and the Meissen and Porvoo Common Statements) that a ministry of pastoral responsibility (*episkope*) is necessary to the unity and apostolic continuity of the Church and is one of its essential tasks.

Pastoral care and oversight are just as much a part of the overall mission of the Church as are the ministry of the word and of the sacraments. It is what the Church is sent to do; one of its constitutive tasks. It is an aspect of the Church's apostolicity. Therefore, we can safely say that there is no Church without genuine *episkope*, though this may be carried out in various forms and by means of various structures (as a recent ecumenical convergence affirms: Bouteneff and Falconer, eds 1999). Where Churches have moved to the step of mutual ecclesial acknowledgement, in the quest for visible unity (as in, for example, the Meissen Agreement between the Church of England and the Evangelical Church of Germany, the Fetter Lane Agreement between the Church of England and the Moravian Church, the Reuilly Agreement between the British and Irish Anglican Churches and the French Lutheran and Reformed Churches and the Anglican–Methodist Covenant for England), acknowledgement of the reality and genuineness of the pastoral oversight of the participating Churches is a vital ingredient. The mutual acknowledgement of Churches as ecclesial bodies entails mutual acknowledgement of the authenticity of their pastoral oversight. To sharpen the point, personal *episkope* is not the same as episcopacy and may exist, paradoxically, in non-episcopal forms.

Another way of putting this point is to say that pastoral responsibility (*episkope*) is necessary to the integrity and unity of the Church. Recent ecumenical agreements have stressed this.

- The progressive agreements forged by Lutheran–Episcopal Dialogue in the United States over past decades, built on mutual acknowledgement of the reality of ordained ministry, including *episkope*, as a stage towards the integration of ministries eventually achieved in *Called to Common Mission* (1999).
- BEM states that 'a ministry of *episkope* is necessary to express and safeguard the unity of the body.' It adds: 'Every church needs this ministry of unity in some form in order to be the Church of God, the one body of Christ, a sign of the unity of all in the Kingdom' (BEM 1982: 23M).
- In accord with the developments in the understanding of the Church's apostolicity that would lead to BEM, the report of the Anglican–Lutheran International Commission (1970–72) affirms that *episkope* or oversight in the matters of doctrine, ordinations and pastoral care 'is inherent in the apostolic character of the Church's life, mission and ministry' (Pullach 1973: para. 79). This is then re-affirmed in the report of the Anglican–Lutheran Consultation on Episcope of 1987, *The Niagara Report* (Niagara 1988: para. 69).
- The Meissen Common Statement between the Church of England and the Evangelical Church in Germany (not an agreement that brings about full ecclesial communion, including the interchangeability of ministries) incorporates this earlier text when it says: 'We believe that a ministry of pastoral oversight (*episkope*), exercised in personal, collegial and communal ways, is necessary to witness to and safeguard the unity and apostolicity of the Church' (Meissen 1992: para. 15, ix).
- The Porvoo Common Statement between the British and Irish Anglican Churches and the Nordic and Baltic Lutheran Churches follows this verbatim and uses it as a building block towards the visible unity of episcopally ordered Churches (Porvoo 1993: 21, para. 32k).

- The report of the Anglican–Methodist international dialogue *Sharing in the Apostolic Communion* (1996) interestingly relates *episkope* to the four credal notes or dimensions of the Church: 'Episcopé [sic] is a gift of the Holy Spirit and involves the maintenance and furtherance of the apostolicity, catholicity, unity and discipline of the Church; it is given to nurture the Church's *koinonia*' (Anglican–Methodist International Commission, 1996, para. 46). The report of the informal conversations between the Church of England and the Methodist Church that led to the establishment of the Formal Conversations that began in 1999, usefully identifies *episkope* as a visible sign of communion (*Commitment to Mission and Unity*, para. 10(d)).

The special character of the pastoral responsibility exercised in the Church has been the subject of continuous reflection on the part of theologians and pastors from the beginning (for general surveys see McNeill 1952 and Evans, ed. 2000). Let us glance at some indicative examples of the theory and practice of pastoral care during the Christian centuries. Pope Gregory the Great produced his *Liber regulae pastoralis* around the turn of the sixth century. It gives food for thought that for over a thousand years it was monasticism that provided the pastoral care of Christian Europe. The Fourth Lateran Council of 1215 produced seventy-one decrees (perhaps the most impressive and far-reaching legislation of any medieval Council until the fifteenth century) providing for rigorous pastoral reform. The decrees affected bishops, priests and laity, directing them to the essential pastoral task. The mendicant orders, the friars, were raised up to meet the pastoral needs of a society ravaged by wars and disasters and fragmented by the social dislocation that accompanied the rise of new urban centres of population. People and priests were decimated by the Black Death in the middle years of the fourteenth century (the Deanery of Kenn in the Diocese of Exeter was possibly the worst affected in England: eighty-six incumbents of its seventeen benefices died in the space of two years).

The Reformation saw a renewal of pastoral ministry and of its theology. For Calvin, it may surprise some to learn, 'neither are the light and heat of the sun, nor meat and drink, so necessary to sustain and cherish the present life as is the apostolical and pastoral office to preserve a Church in the earth' (Calvin 1962: II, 317; IV.iii.2). Beginning in the sixteenth century the Society of Jesus compensated for the limitations of parochial ministry by scholarly teaching and missionary work. To jump to the twentieth century, Franciscans in England, frequently eccentrics, threw in their lot with down-and-outs and in their religious houses they offered 'a parish to the parishless'. They well understood that pastoral care is the heart of evangelism and that to stretch out the hand of friendship predisposes hearts to receive the gospel.

Social disintegration, urbanization, natural and man-made disasters, homelessness, ignorance of the faith, multitudes distanced from the Church – it all sounds rather familiar! The Fourth Lateran Council described priests as *medici animarum*, physicians of the soul, and said that to guide souls was the supreme art. It still is, of course, and the Good Shepherd is still our model. The Church of England's canons sum up the pastoral imperative for the one who has the cure of souls: 'He [sic] shall be diligent in visiting his parishioners, particularly those that are sick and infirm; and he shall provide opportunities whereby any of his parishioners may resort unto him for spiritual counsel and advice' (Canon C 24).

For a modern definition of pastoral care we may turn to Clebsch and Jaeckle's *Pastoral Care in Historical Perspective* (1975). They define it as 'helping acts, done by representative Christian persons, directed towards the healing, sustaining, guiding and reconciling of troubled persons whose troubles arise in the context of ultimate meanings and concerns' (quoted by Pattison 1988: 12). As Pattison himself suggests, this statement is slanted towards the individual and therapeutic aspects of pastoral care. It lacks recognition of the communal and ethical formation that gives pastoral care objectivity and permanence. Pattison therefore offers an alternative definition – one with more theological weight – that sees pastoral care as 'that activity, undertaken especially by representative Christian persons, directed towards the elimination and relief of sin and sorrow and the presentation of all people perfect in Christ to God' (Pattison 1998: 13). In this statement pastoral care is explicitly orientated to Christ's work of salvation. It includes training in discipleship, in holiness, within the community of the Church and through its means of grace.

If communal and ethical formation belongs essentially to pastoral care, then part of the Church's pastoral task is to offer a moral framework for life, one that is grounded in biblical revelation and Christian tradition. Pattison draws on the writings of Don Browning (particularly *The Moral Content of Pastoral Care*, 1976) in which Browning deplores the neglect of norms and values in pastoral care in favour of short-term, reactive therapeutic services. The lack of a common fund of normative religious and ethical meanings and symbols, that set out the good for humankind, contributes to the difficulties that individuals experience in life and is linked to psychological and emotional dysfunction. To provide and inculcate standards, goals and values that are worthy of people's allegiance is, in itself, to make a contribution to their pastoral care (for a discussion of Browning's idea of pastoral care through moral community see Graham 1996: ch. 4: 'Pastoral Care in a Moral Context').

Surely, we might conclude, the Church should offer a vision of the good for humanity, a vision that is compelling for its own members and attractive to people of goodwill who are not fully committed to the Church. It belongs to the moral leadership of the Church to redefine, refocus, and carefully and responsibly critique, if necessary, the consensus of values espoused by society. The Christian perception of the wholeness and fullness of human life, lived in community, is grounded in its doctrines of creation, salvation and the Church, and is articulated in Christian social ethics.

These considerations have implications, however, for how we understand the Church. It is not sufficient to see the congregation simply as a *locus* for liturgical celebration or Christian fellowship or even for service to the community. Undergirding all these is the moral and theological rationale for the Church's existence. The Church stands for and embodies moral values as well as a theological world view. It is, therefore, a place of practical moral reasoning where individuals are helped to 'develop a framework of meanings relevant to all aspects of their life' (Pattison 1988: 37, citing Browning). But, as Alastair MacIntyre has reminded us (e.g., MacIntyre 1985), this framework of meaning, embodied in a community, can only be sustained by a living tradition. Therefore, an essential aim of pastoral care must be to embed individuals in that tradition as it is lived, shaped and reinterpreted in the Church, the moral community that is constituted explicitly by the Christian tradition (including, needless to say, the biblical tradition). The moral challenge that the Church offers is a vital part of its mission.

> Without love, acceptance, forgiveness, there is no healing, no regeneration, no restoration of a broken life or a poisoned relationship. But equally, without a strong moral witness which is willing to affirm goodness and condemn evil, without the courage to risk oneself and one's relationship for a principle a people perish. (J. C. Hoffman, *Ethical Confrontation in Counselling*, 1979, cited in Pattison 1988: 46)

Moral values and ethical principles permeate and undergird the Church's pastoral ministry which is, inescapably, exercised in a social, communal and moral context. These values and principles are articulated in moral discourse in the context of pastoral care, not necessarily directly and confrontationally, but obliquely, questioningly and tentatively. 'Moral discourse does not consist in re-iterating traditional precepts, but in exploring and discussing various important questions' (Pattison 1988: 51). The direct, didactic input will come from the ministry of the word, through preaching and teaching: the personal application that no person can perform appropriately for another, arises through sensitive pastoral care.

The Christian journey begins with initiation into the kingdom of God, through the Church, in baptism, in response to the preaching of the gospel (*kerygma*). It is sustained by the teaching of the word of God (*didache*) and by the Eucharist in the context of Christian fellowship (*koinonia*). It culminates in the eschatological goal of presenting every Christian perfect in Christ to God (Colossians 1.28; cf. Philippians 1.6). At every point, pastoral responsibility forms a vital part of the Church's mission, provided that it is offered (alongside word and sacrament) as a form of evangelization.

Proclaiming the gospel, however eloquently, will cut no ice with unchurched people today unless they are assured by experience that a caring pastoral heart lies beyond the words (see Avis 2003). There is a dynamic interconnection between the ministries of word, sacrament and pastoral care (cf. Clark 1992: 23f.). So let us hear no more of pastoral care as mere 'maintenance' of the status quo, contrasted unfavourably with mission. Effective mission is truly pastoral: it is Christ-like compassionate care that gives mission and evangelization credibility. Pastoral formation, in the sense of making disciples of Jesus Christ, is mandated in the Great Commission and is part of the triple task that Christ wills for his Church within the great *missio dei*.

2

A MINISTRY SHAPED BY THE
MISSION OF GOD

What is and what is not ministry?

'Ministry' is now a seriously overused word. In much that is
written on this subject it is asked to do too much and to
work too hard. There is confusion and uncertainty about
what 'ministry' means as a concept and to whom it applies,
the 'ministers'. Ministry has been called (by Helen
Oppenheimer) a 'greedy concept', one that is imperialistic
and all-absorbing (cited by Hannaford in Hall and
Hannaford, eds 1996: 22). The ambiguous reputation that
'ministry' has begun to acquire is not, of course, the fault of
the word itself (a key New Testament term: *diakonia*) nor of
the various ministers of the Churches. It points rather to a
certain poverty of theological analysis and rigour in this
area on the part of a number of Churches, for whom
ministry is their very lifeblood. The notion of ministry has
become so broad that it is in danger of becoming
meaningless. The lifeblood is beginning to seem rather
anaemic.

There has been an understandable and perfectly proper
reaction against the clericalist tendency that is strong in the
tradition of 'hierarchical' Churches. The clericalist concept
of ministry over-narrowed the meaning of ministry by
restricting it to those who are ordained, to the official work
of the clergy (as in the expression 'going into the ministry'),
so completely disenfranchising the laity as far as ministry is
concerned. But, in the process of liberating ministry from
clericalism, we may have so broadened it that it has no
boundaries. The slogan 'Every member ministry', when

used in a facile way, may signal such a situation. The words 'ministry' and 'minister' are rapidly becoming unserviceable.

In attempting to rehabilitate the term 'ministry' and to reclaim a specific meaning for it, I have two main concerns. The first is to distinguish ministry from the everyday Christian life, the calling to discipleship; the second is to avoid an individualistic and subjective approach to ministry and to reposition it as an essentially ecclesiological concept. Let us take these two issues in order. (At this point I drop the use of inverted commas around ministry.)

In some contexts of usage ministry seems to have become equivalent to everything a Christian does in his or her life of discipleship. Whatever is consecrated to Christ, whatever is done in a spirit of self-offering and out of love for God and humankind is dubbed ministry. If we are not careful, the term 'ministry' can absorb the whole of the Christian life into itself. Then there would be nothing that is not ministry – and the term would have lost all meaning. The *reductio ad absurdum* would be that helping with the washing up becomes ministry! Christ's presence and grace should indeed sanctify all our actions, as George Herbert reminds us in his poem (our hymn) 'Teach me, my God and King, in all things thee to see, And what I do in anything, To do it as for thee' – but that does not mean that every action is properly termed 'ministry'.

The assumptions and expectations that we bring to living the Christian life can guide us here. How do we use the word? Is going to church ministry? Saying one's prayers? Giving to charity? Helping an infirm person to the communion rail? Witnessing at the bus stop to a stranger? We would not normally say so. These are only ministry if ministry is equated with Christian behaviour. These are examples of behaviour that every Christian is expected to exhibit. To worship the Lord and to witness to him belong to the basic calling of all Christians in all circumstances.

Ministry must be something more specific than living the Christian life. These are all private actions in the sense that they are personally motivated; they are not publicly awarded and they are not regarded as an individual's special or unique contribution to the mission of the Church.

However, we can envisage certain circumstances in which all these examples could properly become forms of ministry without devaluing the term.

- If a person was deputed to be the first to arrive at the church for a service in order to unlock the door or turn on the heating, that could be regarded as part of that person's ministry because it would be a person's special responsibility, in relation to the Lord and his people, which others recognized and on which they depended.
- Similarly, if a person, known to be faithful and powerful in prayer, were requested by the Church to uphold a certain project in sustained intercession, and where perhaps, by reason of health or circumstances, that was all they could do, it might be right to see that as their ministry in that context.
- If a wealthy Christian was known as a benefactor to whom the Church could turn expectantly in times of financial need, his or her active generosity could properly be regarded as a ministry.
- If a congregation regularly had a number of infirm or handicapped attenders and some able-bodied members were specifically given the responsibility of seeing that they were helped and supported, what they did could well be considered their ministry.
- Again, if a lay Christian was gifted in personal evangelism and able to form fruitful relationships with people through casual encounters and if sometimes this led eventually to individuals being brought to faith and to take part in the worship of the Church, their gift might

be recognized by their being set free from other Church responsibilities to use it to the full, including at bus stops! Then a gift would become a ministry.

Thinking about normal usage with the help of these examples already suggests some provisional conclusions. Christian actions are acknowledged by us to be expressions of ministry if they are recognized, expected or mandated by the Church, if they have a public dimension and if they are subject to some kind of accountability and oversight. But if they lack these elements they are not examples of ministry but of everyday Christian discipleship. This distinction leads to the second area where greater clarity is required.

The second problem is the individualistic and proprietorial attitude to ministry that is prevalent in the church today. At its most objectionable, it amounts to the self-creation of ministry. Alarmingly subjective assumptions regarding ministry are revealed in such common expressions as 'my ministry' and 'the ministry God has given me'. It is not at all unusual for people to suggest to bishops, clergy and other pastors that the Church should 'recognize their ministry'. These telltale phrases reveal how fundamental the sense of having a ministry is to our personal identity and sense of self-worth. It is very precious to the individual and to feel that it is threatened is deeply painful. The other side of the coin, however, is that there is little awareness among those who fall into using such expressions as 'my ministry' that it is in fact for the Church corporately to discern what their ministry is and to decide how and where it should be exercised – or at least an awareness that this is a joint exercise in which the Church and the individual Christian, the whole and the part, the body and the limb, discern God's will and purpose together.

The truth is that on our own we cannot know what our ministry is: we need the Church to help us to understand the ministry to which we are called. Much Christian activity is merely self-authorized: on my view, that disqualifies it as ministry. Ministry is not whatever an individual feels moved to do for the Lord or to offer to the Church, whether it is needed or not. That way of looking at the matter seems to have things the wrong way round. Ministry is something public and representative, rather than private and individual. It is a set of roles and activities that are thrust upon us, sometimes to our surprise, and perhaps accepted reluctantly at first (a point well made by Dewar in *Called or Collared?*: Dewar 1991). However, the ministry to which we are called by the Holy Spirit through the Church should not be alien to us; our true ministry must be our true *métier*, for God's 'service is perfect freedom' and in laying down our life for Christ's sake we find our true self again.

'My ministry' is not a phrase that I could ever comfortably use. It is not for me to claim it and it is not mine to claim. It is for the Church to say whether there is a ministry there. Even then it remains Christ's ministry in me, something that belongs firmly in the realm of grace, that I can never take possession of, but can only be a channel for: 'not I, but the grace of God that is with me' (1 Corinthians 15.10; cf. Colossians 1.28).

It is not individuals, some of whom may be novices in the faith, who deserve to be rapped across the knuckles for not having a better grasp of the theology of ministry. The fault, if fault there be, lies with our attempt in the Churches to be inappropriately inclusive when we talk about ministry. At this point our language uncritically echoes contemporary culture which prizes non-judgemental tolerance and inclusiveness above everything (Hollenbach 2002: 22–31). Everyone should be included; no one should feel left out! What must be avoided at all costs, according to this politically correct rhetoric, is giving any impression that there are two classes of Christian: those who have ministry and those who do not. It is the false assumption that difference entails a hierarchical value-judgement ('classes') and the questionable desire to obliterate distinctions that leads to the claim that all Christians are by definition ministers.

There is a fundamental theological confusion going on here. It is important to be inclusive where appropriate, but perhaps we are looking in the wrong place, an inappropriate place. It is discipleship, not ministry, that is the inclusive category. In our baptism we are all called equally to be disciples of Christ and promise to follow and obey him. As Bonhoeffer says, to follow Christ is 'the content of discipleship' (Bonhoeffer 1959: 49). In fact it is because we are disciples that we are Christians. In that sense, to say that all Christians are disciples is a tautology: they are so by definition. But it is a tautology that has bite, for the call to discipleship can be renewed, as Peter found after he had betrayed Jesus (John 21.15–19: 'Follow me ... Feed my sheep'). It is a call to go continually further in self-dedication and obedience, as Paul confesses (Philippians 3.14: 'I press on toward the goal for the prize of the heavenly call of God in Christ Jesus'). The first disciples literally followed Jesus on a journey that would lead to the inauguration of the Kingdom (Luke 9.23–27, 57–62). The same people can be both disciples and Apostles, but they cannot be Apostles until they have been disciples (for analysis of discipleship in the Gospel of Mark, see Best 1981).

What becomes of ordination when we claim that all Christians are ministers because they are Christians? Inevitably it is played down: ordination becomes not a particularly big deal. It seems merely to give public recognition to what is already true: that a certain person has certain gifts and that these are to be encouraged and recognized. This is like asking, 'What does marriage add to a couple who are already living together?' or, 'Why kiss your spouse when you both know that you love one another?' The underlying question is: do solemn liturgical actions of a sacramental nature simply celebrate and affirm what is already the case, or do they add something incremental to the situation and move it to a new level? (cf. Hefling 2003). We tackle the question, What does ordination do?, towards the end of this book, but here we can make some preliminary comments that point towards our conclusion.

Certainly all Christians are equal in value in the sight of God. An archbishop with a major public profile is not more precious to God than a lay Christian who minds the children's crèche on Sunday mornings. All contributions to the life and mission of the Church are of equal worth in spiritual terms when they flow from prayerful self-offering to God and God's Church. But perhaps there are certain activities or actions that are more essential to the life of the Church than others and therefore greater care needs to be taken over them and over who performs them.

It has been held generally in the Christian Church that three activities are necessary to the life of the Church in a way that other activities are not – in fact they are so necessary that the Church cannot exist without them. They are ecclesially constitutive. These activities are, of course, the ministry of the word (preaching and teaching), the celebration and administration of the sacraments (primarily but not solely baptism and the Eucharist) and the exercise of pastoral responsibility that underpins these two major expressions of ministry. These are the three primary, public and mandated tasks of the Church, grounded in the Great Commission of Matthew 28.19 to teach, to baptize and to make disciples. Ministry in the Church cannot be something other than the performance of word, sacrament and pastoral care. All ministry must be related to these three interlinked activities. It seems to follow that any activity that cannot be ultimately referenced in this way should not properly be called ministry. Ministry therefore becomes a term of discrimination, involving a value judgement about what is essential to the Church's life and mission, not a catch-all descriptive term for whatever is going on.

'Ministry' in the New Testament

Well-meaning inclusiveness is not wholly to blame for our current lazy thinking about ministry. There is also a theological problem. The interpretation of the New Testament term for ministry, *diakonia*, has contributed to our difficulties. The familiar or received interpretation starts from the apparently straightforward meaning, on the surface of the language, of *diakonia* as service and accordingly emphasizes the servant nature of ministry. Obviously, it is assumed, every Christian is called to love and serve their neighbour: therefore it follows that every Christian has a ministry. Here ministry is equated with the committed or consecrated Christian life. This view tends to locate ministry within the ethical sphere of the moral and social obligations that are incumbent on all Christians at all times. This interpretation of *diakonia* supports the claim that all Christians by definition have a ministry, since all Christians are called to love and serve God and their neighbour. Ministry is in danger of being reduced to a function of the two tables of the Ten Commandments or of our Lord's summary of the law: to love God and one's neighbour.

A variation on this theme is the appeal to the gifts of the Spirit: if all Christians have received a gift, all must have a ministry. Gift and ministry are closely linked in 1 Corinthians 12. Käsemann points out that in 1 Corinthians 12.4–11 ministries (*diakoniai*) seem to be interchangeable with gifts (*charismata*). He draws attention to 1 Corinthians 7.7: 'Each has a particular gift from God . . .' and comments, 'There is no divine gift that does not bring with it a task' (Käsemann 1964: 65). Schweizer, similarly, appeals to the gifts of the Spirit in the Pauline letters and concludes: 'Everyone, therefore, without exception, is given his ministry' (Schweizer 1961: 100). Barrett goes down the same road, equating membership with ministry in Paul's theology: 'The first thing to be said about the ministry in the Pauline epistles is that every member of the church was a minister.' However, it immediately becomes apparent that Barrett is using ministry as a virtual synonym for function: 'every member of the church had, in Paul's view, like every member of the human body, its own function' (Barrett 1985: 31). 'Function' is unashamedly the rubric under which Barrett discusses ministry in Paul.

But the texts that Schweizer, Käsemann and Barrett cite do not necessarily substantiate the argument that to be a Christian is to have a ministry (see also the careful discussion in Thiselton 2000: 928–33). The gambit does not make sense unless gift is exactly equated with ministry – have gift, have ministry – and ministry is regarded as simply a function.

If the terms *charisma* and *diakonia* were completely interchangeable, the crucial term *diakonia* on which so much pivots in Paul's understanding of his mission, would be redundant. In fact, like much parallelism in the Hebrew Bible and particularly in the Pauline letters, the parallelism is not univocal; it is a differentiated and perhaps even incremental parallelism. There are significant differences of nuance between the parallel phrases 'gifts', 'ministries' and 'activities' (as the NRSV translates them), even though they are not referring to three completely separate areas. However, these Protestant scholars have a valid point; they are not simply making ideological use of the doctrine of 'the priesthood of all believers' in the interests of ecclesiastical egalitarianism. Paul does envisage a community where ideally all have a ministry because all have gifts which are both consecrated by the individual and recognized by the Church. My contention is simply – and radically – that this equation of gift and ministry is not automatic and should not be presumed in the case of every individual Christian.

There is, however, an alternative approach to the interpretation that equates *diakonia* with service. The revisionist interpretation of this key New Testament term *diakonia*/ministry emphasizes the element of commissioning and responsible agency. Fresh study of the *diakon-* cluster of words in their classical context and in the New Testament suggests that it refers to the carrying out of a commission on behalf of someone in authority (Collins 1990). In the Christian sense, therefore, ministry is not so much something that we offer to do for others as something that God has laid upon us. And it is not so much a general attitude of service, but a specific task for which we are mandated. Ministry is representative of higher authority. Therefore it has to be specifically awarded. It cannot be assumed, or claimed as of right. This view therefore challenges the consensus in current thinking about ministry that all Christians are *ex officio* ministers through baptism (Collins 1992). This interpretation obviously lends itself to a narrowing of the meaning of ministry. Ministry is found where there is authoritative commissioning and responsible agency on behalf of another, either in the form of ordination or in some other way. John Calvin errs on the right side when he translates Romans 12.7: 'Let him who is ordained as a minister exercise his office in ministering' (Calvin 1961: 269), so presupposing that there is no ministry without some kind of ordering, commissioning or formal recognition.

Collins's negative answer to the question he poses – Are all Christians ministers? – contains more than a grain of truth, but in my view it goes too far. While I would certainly want to affirm the element of commissioning, representation and responsible agency in ministry, I think the conclusion, to which the logic of Collins's argument points, that most Christians therefore do not or cannot have a ministry, is unacceptable and unbiblical. All Christians have received a charisma of the Holy Spirit through their initiation into the body of Christ. Every limb or organ of the body of Christ has a vital role for the well-being of the whole body (1 Corinthians 12). All baptized believers are potential ministers. All are called to minister in one way or another. But that call needs to be issued and received. When their ministry is recognized and owned by the community (in tacit and informal ways, as well as in explicit and formal ones), they are seen to act in the name of Christ's Church.

What we need to guard against is not the idea that every baptized Christian can and should have a ministry, but the twin notions that everything that a Christian does, in dedication to the Lord, is ministry and that the individual decides what their ministry is. The scenario to strive for, I believe, is where every active member of a Christian community has a defined role within which they exercise their God-given gifts and this is recognized, tacitly or explicitly by the Christian community. Then St Paul's image of the body working together in every limb and organ (1 Corinthians 12.12–31; Ephesians 4.4–16) becomes a reality. These communities, are, I imagine, not uncommon. The congregations of the parishes near Exeter where I ministered for many years were like that. Almost everyone had a recognized contribution to make. There were hardly any 'passengers' – though these were true parishes, not gathered churches. The congregations were effectively dispersed throughout the wider local community and kept open boundaries with them.

Ministry in focus

Thomas O'Meara, a Roman Catholic theologian, has proposed a useful definition of Christian ministry. He suggests that ministry should be defined as *'the public activity of a baptized follower of Jesus Christ flowing from the Spirit's charism and an individual personality on behalf of a Christian community to witness to, serve and realize the kingdom of God'* (O'Meara 1983: 142, my italics). Let us pause to analyse this statement and to elaborate what it is claiming.

First, ministry is a 'public' matter, not a private matter. This must mean that ministry involves a public dimension, not that everything that is ministry must be performed in full public view. A minister preparing a sermon in the study is no less ministry because no one sees it happen. It is public because it is publicly expected and will be publicly received and publicly evaluated.

Second, ministry is 'activity', it is not merely a state of being. Although what a minister is and is called to become as a person is crucial, their inner state is known to God and is not open to public scrutiny. It is often said that the ordained are called to *be* and this is a valuable emphasis if it counteracts activism – self-justification through frenzied activity of an ecclesiastical sort, activism that conceals an inner hollowness, emptiness and self-doubt and lack of reliance on the calling and promises of God. But *being* on its own is not ministry, because ministry is not a passive state but an active one. It receives concrete expression in carrying out the tasks for which it is commissioned.

Third, ministry is undertaken by 'a baptised follower of Jesus Christ'. Baptism is, as we shall emphasize later, the foundation of ministry. Ministry can flow only from our identification with the death and resurrection of Christ and his gift of the Spirit. Just as the Spirit was given 'without measure' to Jesus as the Christ or Messiah, anointing him as Prophet, Priest and King, so the Spirit is given to those who are baptized into him and share in his threefold messianic identity as a royal prophetic priesthood (see further below). Ministry is not, however, simply an outworking of baptism or a direct expression of it. That would be discipleship, dying with Christ and rising with him to newness of life so that we may heed his call to follow him day by day. Something more is needed, something that is given in ordination or some other liturgical commissioning or form of recognition by the Church. We might say that to be a baptized disciple of Jesus Christ is a necessary but not a sufficient condition for ministry.

Fourth, ministry flows from 'the Spirit's charism'. Although, as I have argued, ministry is much more than the exercise of a spiritual gift, it does belong wholly within the realm of gift, of grace. The great fundamental and all-determining gift is that of God's Son. 'The *charisma* of God is eternal life in Christ Jesus our Lord' (Romans 6.23). *Charismata* are free gifts or gifts that flow from grace. Barrett brings out Paul's play on words in Romans 12.6 when he translates: '. . . we have *gifts* of *grace* differing according to the *grace* God has *given* us' (Barrett 1962: 237, my italics). This resonates with Ephesians 4.7: 'Each of us was given grace according to the measure of Christ's gift.' Grace, gift and *diakonia* are also linked in 1 Peter 4.10 where *diakonountes* should be translated 'ministering', not 'serving'. The AV gets it right, against the NRSV and REB: 'As every man hath received the gift, even so minister the same to one another, as good stewards of the manifold grace of God.'

Ministry depends utterly on the power of the Holy Spirit, on the spiritual anointing that we receive not only in baptism and in confirmation, but more relevantly in ordination and no doubt in other forms of commissioning. We are strengthened to meet every God-sent challenge. At the same time, we offer our natural gifts, those of our personality, character, aptitudes and skills, both natural and acquired, so that these may be consecrated, purified and raised to a higher level by the grace of the Spirit. The process of discernment regarding the appropriate ministry for any one of us involves evaluating both our natural gifts and talents and our openness to these being sanctified and shaped by the Holy Spirit and channelled into the forms of ministry that the Church, in prayerful dependence on God's guidance, steers us into. 'Ministry is the proper and normal expression of *charism* in the life of the Church ... the public and communally recognised form of *charism*' (Hannaford in Hall and Hannaford, eds 1996: 51).

Fifth, ministry is on behalf of 'a Christian community'. Ministry is undertaken on behalf of a particular Church, but by virtue of that, it is undertaken on behalf of the whole

Church. Ministerial actions have the formal intention 'to do what the Church does'. That is why Churches ordain their clergy 'to the office and work of a deacon/priest/bishop in the Church of God'. There cannot be a ministry that relates merely to 'a Christian community' but not to the Christian community, the Church as such. Ministry is evoked by the Church, recognized by the Church, shaped by it and accountable to it. Ministry qualifies as ministry when the Church somehow gives cognizance to it.

Clearly ministry is not embraced or exercised on our own behalf, but on behalf of the Church. So what is the Church here? It is surely both the Church of Christ – one, holy, catholic and apostolic – and the local Church (which participates in these attributes of the universal Church). The local Church is delimited by the scope of pastoral responsibility and the reach of oversight. In episcopally ordered Churches, the oversight concerned is that of the bishop and the local Church is therefore the diocese. Churches that are not ordered episcopally have their own forms of oversight together with structures to fit. The important point is that ministry is not exercised only on behalf of the congregation to which the minister belongs, but on behalf of the wider Church, particularly that form of it within which the oversight of the minister is located, and ultimately on behalf of the whole Church, in both its mystical nature as the Body of Christ and its visible, empirical manifestation as the universal Church.

But could there be genuine ministries that are not owned, seemingly not wanted by the Church? This possibility cannot be excluded since the Church on earth is not infallible in the administration of its ministry. Given the importance of spiritual gifts, I think we have to allow that some 'ministries', especially of a prophetic kind, may not be recognized by the Church at the time, and may be disputed or even rejected. They may, however, be seen in retrospect to have been distinguished ministries, e.g. Thomas Aquinas and Martin Luther, George Fox and John Wesley. (I write this in a house where persecuted 'Friends' – Quakers – secretly welcomed George Fox on at least one occasion; I put the finishing touches around the time of the signing of the Anglican–Methodist Covenant for England.)

Finally, ministry is given 'to witness to, serve and realize the Kingdom of God'. Ministry is placed at the service of the Kingdom of God and is set in the light of the Kingdom. Volumes have been written about the meaning of the Kingdom of God in the Bible and particularly in the teaching of Jesus. Essentially, the Kingdom is the reign of God, God's sovereign authority acknowledged and obeyed in the world and in our lives. That authority is exercised in relation to a purpose that, in the Christian understanding, is revealed as a purpose of love, grace and goodness. The Kingdom is advanced when human life, with all its repercussions in the created order, is brought under the sway of God's rule. When we set ministry before the face of the Kingdom, we acknowledge that it plays a part in bringing to pass God's purpose for the world, a purpose that is Christ-centred and is described in Scripture as being to reconcile and unite all things in Christ (Colossians 1.20; Ephesians 1.10).

Another language for this fundamental orientation of ministry to the purposes of God is the language of *missio dei*, which we have expounded in the first part of this book. The *missio dei* is to bring about God's Kingdom of love and peace, justice and freedom, in and through Jesus Christ. So to relate ministry to the Kingdom is to underline the point that ministry is shaped by mission because the mission to which the Church is called takes the form of a ministry. St Paul saw his apostolate as an integral part of God's action in Christ for the reconciliation of the world. God had acted to reconcile the world in Christ. The Apostle besought humankind to be reconciled to God through Christ. His ministry was an indispensable part of God's mission (Kruse 1983: 178).

The Kingdom of God forms the ultimate horizon for ministry. This suggests that the core tasks of ministry (the word, the sacraments and pastoral care) are the activities that build the Kingdom. If we want to see the Kingdom come in our midst (as we pray in the Lord's Prayer), we should look to those ministries. The Kingdom is not something ready-made that will descend from heaven shimmering in our midst. It is not some exotic creation that bears no relation to the daily tasks of the Church. Though it is greater than the Church, will always transcend it and should not be identified without remainder with the Church, there is no Kingdom without the Church. The Church is structurally internal to the Kingdom. The vital tools that build the Kingdom of God are precisely the powerful preaching of the gospel, the faithful teaching of the apostolic faith, the assiduous administration of baptism and celebration of the Eucharist, and the conscientious and skilled exercise of pastoral responsibility (including feeding the hungry, healing the sick and bringing justice to the oppressed).

When O'Meara ends his definition of ministry by relating it to the Kingdom of God, his argument cuts two ways. It both relativizes ministry and puts it in its place, as it were, cutting it down to size, in case our high calling as ministers of the gospel should go to our heads, and at the same time it exalts ministry by drawing out its crucial role in salvation history and the ultimate redemptive plan of God when God will be all in all (1 Corinthians 15.28).

After setting down, with O'Meara's help, the basic essentials of ministry, I am ready to offer my own more concise working definition of ministry that is intended to take us away from the spurious all-inclusive and individualistic understandings of ministry that are pervasive today, and bring out instead its reconstructed meaning. My proposed definition is: *Ministry is God-given work for the cause of God that is acknowledged by the Church.* That is to say, ministry takes place when a person, whether lay or ordained, performs a role or task on behalf of the Christian community which the community recognizes as its own work. Let me offer a few points of clarification of the approach I am advocating.

First: ministry is missiological through and through. It is not confined to the 'internal' life of the congregation (say in worship, teaching or administration), but is given in the service of God's Kingdom far and wide. Ministry is therefore shot through with a missionary imperative. Because mission takes the form of a ministry, ministry must be shaped by mission. All too often we see ministry, ordained or lay, that is almost entirely orientated to the internal life of the Church – wholly taken up with the round of perfectly proper services for the faithful few and with organizing worthy activities for those within the fold. An increasingly familar scenario is that of fewer and fewer clergy rushing about faster and faster for more and more congregations that are getting smaller and smaller. Ministry on those lines is not consciously directed to those in God's world who are not yet members of the Church and have not yet received the gift of faith, but who might attain both these things if they were proactively offered the word and the sacraments in the setting of evident pastoral care. We sense that this is a seriously deficient ministry, one that has become distorted and one that is in danger of becoming futile.

Second: if commissioning or recognition by the Church is a condition of ministry, so that it can truly be said that ministry does what the Church does, we need a serviceable and realistic understanding of that recognition. In fact the community can take cognizance of ministry in various ways, tacitly and informally as well as explicitly and formally. There is something like a sliding scale here, from solemn liturgical actions, such as ordination, at one end to an informal understanding that emerges within a parish or congregation, at the other.

Third: though ministry must be acknowledged in some way by the Church, it is not the Church's creation. It is crucially God's call that makes someone a minister, not the Church's liturgy. Ultimately, it is God who ordains or commissions, through the Church (Bradshaw in Holeton *et al.* 1997: 9). Ministry has a divine, not merely a human mandate. The Holy Trinity is the source of ministry and gives gifts for this purpose (1 Corinthians 12. 4–7).

Fourth: while emphasizing the role of the community in authorizing ministry, we know that it does not make any kind of theological sense to separate Christ and his Church. He is at work in his Body through the Spirit. As 1 Corinthians 12.6 puts it: 'There are varieties of activity, but in all of them and in everyone the same God is active' (REB). The Church has a vital role in this commissioning. The calling to ministry may be initiated by the Church and responded to by the individual. Or it may be initiated in the individual and confirmed by the Church. The Spirit works in the individual as a part of the Body and through the Body in relation to the individual. But either way, the Holy Spirit is the author of ministry.

The ministry of Christ

The most crucial truth about Christian ministry, whether ordained or lay, is that it is the ministry of Jesus Christ. This principle is the alpha and omega of the Church's doctrine of ministry. The first Doctrine Commission of the Church of England, which sat from 1922 to 1938, began its account of the ministry with the words: 'The fundamental Christian ministry is the ministry of Christ. There is no Christian priesthood or ministry apart from his' (Doctrine Commission 1938: 114). The only way in which we can make theological sense of ministry is to see it as an expression of the ministry of Jesus Christ through his Church. There is no ministry apart from his and outside of his. All ministry is simply Christ at work through the presence of the Holy Spirit, leading, teaching and sanctifying his body through human – unworthy and inadequate human – instruments. The ministry of Jesus Christ in the Church is the form taken by his mission in the world, *missio Christi*. The mission of Christ in turn flows from the *missio dei*.

Because human ministry is a channel for Christ, the King who gives himself to God in total self-offering, it embodies both authority and the spirit of self-giving. This applies to both lay and ordained ministry. Lay ministry as well as ordained ministry is Christ's. Jesus the carpenter was a lay person, not a professional religious figure, not a Pharisee or a Scribe. Ordained ministry is also Christ's, but it should retain the spirit of Jesus the carpenter. To be a carpenter was then (and still is now) a worthwhile and respected occupation, that of a skilled artisan with a recognized place in the community. But a carpenter does not expect to be the centre of attraction, to enjoy the attentions of the media, to receive adulation or to exhibit a charismatic personality. The spirit of quiet competence and of steady dedication to the task is probably more typical of the carpenter's approach to his work.

Because the ministry, whether that of a lay person or of an ordained person, is essentially that of Jesus Christ, it is not fundamentally compromised by human weakness and failure. Article XXVI of the Thirty-Nine Articles affirms that because the clergy act in the name of Christ and by his commission and authority and because he has given his promises to his Church, 'the unworthiness of the ministers hinders not the effect of the sacrament'. With the eyes of faith we see beyond the human instrument, which will always be both inadequate and unworthy, to Christ himself, the Minister (*diakonos*) of God. It is Christ who speaks his own scriptural word in preaching and teaching, washes our sins from us in baptism, gives himself to us in the forms of bread and wine, and guides and supports us through the pastoral care that the ministers of the Church provide. Through human ministers we receive Christ's touch on our lives.

- Because only God can speak God's creative word to the deepest heart and mind of the individual (Hebrews 4.12), we must say that Christ is the true minister of the word. Any human ministry of the word can only be a infinitely fragmentary participation in Christ the Logos (Word) of God who reveals and communicates the Father to the created order (John 1.1–14; Hebrews 1.1–3a).
- Because only Christ can unite us to himself in an act of prevenient grace, the grace that precedes our human response (Romans 6.3–11; 8.29–30; Ephesians 2.4–10; 1 John 4.10), we can affirm that Christ is the true minister of the sacrament of baptism.
- Because only the Good Shepherd can call his sheep by name and lead them forth (John 10.3–4), we must believe that Christ is the minister of pastoral care (1 Peter 2.25: 'the Shepherd and Bishop of your souls'; 5.2–4: under shepherds and 'the Chief Shepherd').

The sixteenth-century Reformers emphasized in concrete and realistic terms that Christ is the minister of word and sacrament. Luther says in his *Large Catechism*: 'To be baptized in God's name is to be baptized not by men but by God himself. Although it is performed by men's hands, it is nevertheless truly God's own act' (Tappert, ed. 1959: 437). Cranmer says of the ministry of the word:

> The minister of the church speaketh unto us God's own words, which we must take as spoken from God's mouth, because from that mouth it came, and his word it is, and not the minister's.

The same applies to the sacraments, continues Cranmer:

> Likewise, when he ministereth to our sights Christ's holy sacraments, we must think Christ crucified and presented before our eyes, because the sacraments so represent him, and be his sacraments, and not the priest's.

Applied to baptism this means:

> as the priest putteth his hand to the child outwardly, and washeth him with water, so must we think that God putteth to his hand inwardly, and washeth the infant with his Holy Spirit; and moreover, that Christ himself cometh down upon the child, and apparelleth him with his own self.

And with regard to Holy Communion, Cranmer concludes, just as the priest administers the bread and wine to feed the body, so by the eyes of faith we behold Christ nourishing both body and soul unto eternal life (Cranmer, P.S., I, p. 366, cited Dugmore 1958: 188).

The truth that Christian ministry is the ministry of Christ himself links ministry with baptism. Ministry is grounded in baptism because baptism is the foundational sacrament of the Church. In baptism we are irrevocably and eternally united with Christ. Baptism is given by grace: it is one of God's greatest gifts to us. Our proper response to the grace and gifts of God is one of faith and faith is therefore intrinsic to baptism. However, baptism is not primarily an expression of the faithful human response to the gospel. It is not, as has sometimes been suggested, 'the sacrament of Christian response'. Baptism is not something that we perform; it is not a 'work'. Baptism is something that we receive and that we undergo. Not that baptism should be separated from faith. It is always performed in the context of the confession of faith, though this takes different forms in different traditions, depending whether they practise infant baptism or only 'believer's baptism'. There is no ministry that is not related to our baptism. That is not to say that baptism is a sufficient basis for all forms of ministry or that ordination or some other formal commissioning adds nothing to baptism: the fact that a person has been baptized does not in itself entitle them to set themselves up as a minister. But it is to recognize that through baptism and its appropriation through the whole process of Christian initiation (including instruction, Confirmation and Holy Communion) Christians are united with Christ and particularly with him in his death and resurrection. Therefore it is, in the first place, the reality of baptism that enables us to say that ministry is the ministry of Christ in us.

Through the sacrament of baptism, in both its outward obedient performance and its inward dynamic meaning, Christians are united to Christ in his sacrificial death and risen life (Romans 6.3–11). Through this union we share in his anointing by the Holy Spirit at his own baptism (Mark 1.9–11). He received this anointing not as a private individual, since he did not need to undergo the baptism of repentance for the forgiveness of sins, but as representative or corporate person, the personification of Israel, that is to say the Church of God. Jesus was designated Son of God as he rose from the waters of the Jordan and immediately underwent testing in the wilderness for forty days, just as Israel passed through the waters of the Red Sea and was in the wilderness for forty years (Matthew 3.13–17; 4.1–2). His baptism and ours are one indissoluble reality.

Like baptism, ministry also is given by grace; it is not a human achievement, not a 'work'. As a God-sent commission and divinely entrusted task, ministry is thrust upon us. It never becomes our own to dispose of and is not our 'right' to claim. Just as baptism is something that we receive and undergo, so ministry is something that we receive and undertake. The stole worn by ordained priests has been seen as representing the yoke of Christ: 'Take my yoke upon you and learn from me; for I am gentle and humble in heart and you will find rest for your souls. For my yoke is easy and my burden is light' (Matthew 11.29–30). As Bonhoeffer pointed out in *The Cost of Discipleship*, the yoke is easy only for those who willingly submit to it; the burden is light only for those who gladly shoulder it. For those who strive to make them into a 'work', a personal achievement to glory in, Christ's yoke and burden are oppressive (Bonhoeffer 1959: 31). Ministry is received in grace.

There is a parallel between baptism and ordination in the combination of what we do (the 'matter') and what we say (the 'form'). Just as baptism is a God-given sign to which God's promises are joined, and is therefore a sacrament of the Church, so the act of ordination may be described as an ecclesial sign – a performative action that expresses the calling and purpose of the Church and bears witness to that publicly. It is a sign to which the Church attaches prayers that the Holy Spirit will accompany the work of the ordained person with his blessing. In that sense, ordination is a sacramental act (though not necessarily a 'dominical sacrament of the gospel', one explicitly instituted by Christ himself, like baptism and the Eucharist, though some Churches hold that it is) and it makes sense to regard it as a sacrament.

Prophet, Priest and King

Jesus's baptism in the Holy Spirit at the Jordan signifies his messianic identity as the one anointed by God (Mark 1.9–11; Matthew 3.16–17; Luke 3.21–22; Isaiah 42.1; Psalm 2.2,7). This identity is threefold: as Messiah (Christ) he is Prophet, Priest and King – the three Old Testament types of the Messiah who were themselves anointed with the Spirit of God (for an exhaustive analysis of the biblical texts see Grabbe 1995). Unquestionably priests were anointed with oil (Exodus 29.7; 40.13–15; Leviticus 8.12; Psalm 133) as certainly kings were (1 Samuel 15.1; 1 Kings 1.39; 19.15–16; 2 Kings 9.3; Psalm 89.20). Sometimes scholars insist that prophets were not anointed and that therefore the typology is twofold not threefold; but this is to adopt a rather literalistic stance. The anointing is primarily pneumatological (endued with the Spirit) and secondarily physical (anointed with oil). The physical (or sacramental, as we might say) anointing signifies that the Spirit rests permanently upon a person, rather than visiting that person intermittently (1 Samuel 16.13; cf. 2 Samuel 23.2) – which is not to say, of course, that the Spirit could not be withdrawn as a result of divine displeasure (1 Samuel 16.14; Psalm 51.11).

In the Old Testament, priests and kings are normally physically anointed; prophets only rarely. But prophets, like priests and kings, are endued with the power of the Spirit of Yahweh and are thus at least metaphorically anointed (perhaps in 1 Chronicles 16.22). Exceptionally they are also physically anointed. The metaphorical usage would not make sense unless there were a known physical usage that also applied to prophets. Elijah is told by Yahweh to anoint Elisha as his successor. When he finds Elisha he in fact casts his mantle over him: it is implied that he anoints him with oil, but the anointing may be meant metaphorically: it is not described (1 Kings 19.16,19). The Servant of Yahweh in Deutero-Isaiah testifies to his anointing with the spirit of God for a prophetic task: 'to bring good news ... to proclaim liberty ... to proclaim jubilee ... and the day of vengeance ... to comfort ...' (Isaiah 61.1–2). The prophet-servant is the highest type of the Messiah in the Old Testament because he is patently also a priestly and a kingly figure: as priest he makes intercession for the transgressors (Isaiah 53.12), being actually both priest and sacrifice; as king he brings forth and establishes justice among the nations (Isaiah 42.1–4; cf. 9.6f.; 11.2).

PROPHET

As Prophet, Jesus Christ reveals the Father: his nature as love and his redemptive purpose. He does this in his words and deeds (Acts 10.38), but above all in his person and character, which is transparent to God: 'He who has seen me has seen the Father' (John 14.9). Jesus is shown by Luke as identifying with the prophets (Luke 4.24) and in John he is on several occasions recognized as a prophet by others (John 4.19; 6.14;

9.17). He is our one Teacher from whom we learn in a lifelong process of discipleship (Matthew 23.8; 11.29). He continues his prophetic ministry today through the Holy Spirit who in former times, as the Creed puts it, 'spoke through the prophets' and now teaches the Church the mind and heart of Christ and testifies of sin, righteousness and judgement in the world (John 14.16; 16.8–11, 13; 1 Corinthians 2.10). Jesus is the Prophet of Prophets (cf. Acts 3.22) and the end of prophecy in the high canonical sense because in him God is bearing witness to himself and not to another. 'Long ago God spoke to our ancestors in many and various ways by the prophets, but in these last days he has spoken to us by a Son ... the exact imprint of God's very being' (Hebrews 1.1–3). Though in one sense he is the end of prophecy, in another sense he is its fountainhead and beginning, for he brings into being a prophetic people and causes each one of them to share in his prophetic anointing.

PRIEST

As Priest, Jesus Christ offers himself to the Father as an atoning sacrifice, effecting reconciliation between human-kind and God, between God and humankind (Romans 3.24–25; Hebrews 4.14; 8–10). He is at one and the same time the priest who offers sacrifice, the sacrifice that is offered and the altar on which it is offered. The allegorically minded early Fathers were not astray in seeing Jesus's circumcision as the first shedding of his blood. Luke, the only Evangelist to mention the circumcision (Luke 2.21) – if the text is authentic – also records that Jesus's sweat was like great drops of blood falling on the ground in the Garden of Gethsemane (Luke 22.44). His whole mortal life, from infancy to the tomb, is one of total self-oblation to God's redemptive purpose (Hebrews 5.7–10). His once-for-all self-offering continues as he makes intercession for us (Hebrews 7.25) and gathers us into the movement of his self-offering, a ministry in heaven that is reflected on earth in the Eucharist. He is the great high priest, the priest of priests, the end of priesthood and yet its beginning, since he brings into being a priestly people and imparts to each one of them his priestly anointing.

KING

As King, Jesus embodies the reign or Kingdom of God in his person and ministry, inaugurating it here and now in word and deed (Mark 1.15; Luke 4.21; Matthew 10.7; 12.28). His Kingdom is not of (or from) this world: the world did not originate it and cannot account for it or understand it (John 18.36). His Kingdom is eschatological: it is hidden and grows secretly but will one day be revealed. Its fulfilment will be in God's eternal purpose, to which it is subordinate and of which it is, as it were, an instrument (1 Corinthians 15.24). Jesus is Lord of all (Acts 10.36) and that means Lord of the Church too, for he is the head of the body (Ephesians 4.15–16; Colossians 2.19). His eschatological rule is anticipated in the Church because that is where his reign is acknowledged and confessed, though it remains obscured by human sin and blindness even there: the body is not fully in tune with the head. He is King of Kings and the end of all power and authority. At the same time he is the beginning and source of true rule, power and authority (*arche*: 1 Corinthians 15.24; Ephesians 1.21; Colossians 2.10) and has brought into being a kingly, royal people, enduing each one of them with his royal anointing.

United with Christ in baptism and through that sacrament endued with the same Spirit (1 Corinthians 12.13), we ourselves are incorporated into his threefold messianic office. The Church is a prophetic, priestly and royal (kingly) people (1 Peter 2.4–10). It is the Spirit-filled and Spirit-bearing body of Christ (1 Corinthians 3.16; Ephesians 4.4–16). This, not simply the general gift of the

Holy Spirit, is the particular signifiance of the anointing, the use of chrism, at baptism. The *Apostolic Tradition* of Hippolytus (early third century) provides this blessing when the holy oil is brought in at a baptism: 'As thou sanctifiest this oil, so grant to those who use and receive and enjoy it health and strength, just as thou didst in former times to the kings, priests and prophets whom thou didst anoint' (Wainwright 1997: 112; see also on this theme Newman 1990; Wood 2000: 16–19; Goergen in Goergen and Garrido, eds 2000: ch. 9).

Numbered among his people, incorporated into his mystical body, we individually as well as collectively participate in his messianic ministry. As *prophets* we discern and proclaim the word of God, witness to Jesus and confess his name. As *priests* we offer spiritual sacrifices of prayer, praise, gifts and ultimately ourselves. As a *royal* priesthood we play our part in the governance of Christ's kingdom since the duty of kings and queens is to reign. This is the privilege of lay and ordained alike, for baptism incorporates us into the community that is called to ministry. The great original triple calling is that of the Church: our individual callings are simply notes in a vast symphony.

Representative ministry

How can ministry be the ministry of Christ when it is carried out by human instruments? The human instrumentality, which is sinful and fallible, surely must prevent Christ freely working through his Spirit? No minister who is not completely swollen with spiritual pride could say, while preaching or administering the sacraments, 'This is Christ.' But, on the other hand, no minister worth his or her salt could carry on for a moment unless they could truly say, 'Thank God, the people are not receiving me (in these words, in these elements, in this pastoral counsel); they are somehow receiving Christ.'

This paradox that is intrinsic to ministry – that it is divine yet also human, that it is simultaneously Christ yet not only Christ – can be handled if ministry is seen as *representative* of Christ and his Church. Representation is the bridging concept. Representatives stand for the person or institution whom they represent without being that person. They speak and act on behalf of something greater than themselves that awards them the authority to do so. They do not take the place of or substitute for whoever they represent, for that person's mind and will are present in the words and acts of their representative. A representative bears the persona of the one he or she represents. Yet without that mandate the representative is nothing.

Representativeness in ministry is shaped by the paradigm of Jesus Christ, the representative both of the Father and of the human race, especially of the redeemed.

Jesus can be the representative of the Father, not only because he is elect and called (as we see so clearly in his baptismal epiphany), but because he is intimately in tune with the Father's mind and will. From childhood he enjoyed divine favour on account of his holy wisdom (Luke 2.52) and at his baptism this divine good-pleasure too was attested to him by a visual and aural epiphany: 'You are my beloved Son in whom I am well pleased' (Mark 9.11). In his public ministry Jesus was assured of this intimate communion and the revelation that it brought: 'no one knows the Son except the Father, and no one knows the Father except the Son and anyone to whom the Son chooses to reveal him' (Matthew 11.27). He abides in the Father's love because he is implicitly obedient to his commandments (John 15.10). Father and Son indwell one another in truth and love (John 17, especially vv. 20–23).

Jesus is also the representative of humanity and of Israel. His representative significance runs through his life and death, his active and passive obedience as man to the Father's will. This is brought out in the gospels and especially in Paul. Of the four Evangelists, it is Matthew particularly who portrays Jesus, from the infancy narratives onwards, as the embodiment of Israel, the representative Israel. Jesus himself, in consciously identifying with the Servant of Yahweh of Second Isaiah, identifies with a biblical figure who is patently both individual and collective, a powerfully representative symbol. Paul sees Jesus Christ as the last Adam, the perfectly human one, who gathers up the human race in a representative capacity and presents it perfected to the Father (1 Corinthians 15.22–24; cf. Romans 5.12–19). As Dunn says, 'The key idea that runs through Paul's christology and links it to his soteriology is that of solidarity or representation' (Dunn, in Sykes, ed. 1991: 36).

A key Greek word conveying the idea of representation is *huper*, arguably best translated into English as 'on behalf of'. The force of the Greek is obscured in most translations – AV, NRSV, REB – by the weaker preposition 'for', as in 'One has died *for* all, therefore all have died' (2 Corinthians 5.14). Once again there is a symmetry and a sequence connecting what Christ has done for us and what he has called us to do for him. He dies as his people's representative that they may become representatives of him. There is a mutual act of identification. The following slightly cumbersome translation brings out the force of the Greek:

> One has died on behalf of all, therefore all have died. And he died on behalf of all, so that those who live might live no longer for themselves, but on behalf of him who died and was raised on behalf of them ... So we are ambassadors on Christ's behalf, as though God were making his appeal through us; we entreat you on behalf of Christ, be reconciled to God. On our behalf he made him to be sin who knew no sin, so that we might become the righteousness of God in him. (2 Corinthians 5.14–15, 20–21)

Barrett, whose commentary influences the above translation of the *huper*-rich passage in 2 Corinthians, notes: 'On the one hand, Paul has no importance, no message of his own. He does not act on his own behalf, but Christ's ... On the other hand, where Paul is at work, Christ, whom he represents, is at work; where Paul speaks, God speaks. The same act that effected reconciliation, committed to Paul the word and ministry of reconciliation' (Barrett 1973: 178).

The Lord's ambassadors, whether they are the Apostles, the Seventy or the ministers of the Church, stand (proportionately) in the same relation to him as he does to the Father. 'Whoever listens to you listens to me, and whoever rejects you rejects me, and whoever rejects me rejects the one who sent me' (Luke 10.16). 'As the Father has sent me, so I send you' (John 20.21). The ministry of reconciliation that is entrusted to the Church is an outworking of the great act of reconciliation that God accomplished in Christ. That makes the apostolic ministers 'ambassadors for Christ', God making his appeal through them as part of the *missio dei* (2 Corinthians 5.18–20). There is both symmetry and sequence in this twofold relation that Jesus bears, to the Father and to his Apostles. Jesus says in his high priestly prayer, 'As you have sent me into the world, so I have sent them into the world' (John 17.18).

Who represents whom?

Whom or what do ministers represent: Christ or the Church or both? Catholics in various traditions have wanted to stress that the minister (i.e. priest) represents or stands for Christ, especially when presiding at the Eucharist: he ministers *in persona Christi*. St Thomas Aquinas used the expression both of the bishop acting as chief pastor of the diocese and of aspects of the priest presiding at the Eucharist. But Aquinas also saw the priest acting *in persona ecclesiae* in two ways: in leading the Church's profession of faith and in expressing the worship of the congregation (Power 1992).

Evangelicals have been suspicious of this identification, seeing it as the thin (or perhaps thick) end of a sacerdotal wedge implying that lay Christians do not represent Christ in any sense. Evangelicals have preferred, therefore, to think of the ordained minister as speaking for Christ when preaching the word (*in persona Christi?*) and perhaps also as the mouthpiece of the congregation in worship (*in persona ecclesiae?*).

Both the Catholic and the Evangelical traditions are at risk of ending up with an attenuated doctrine of representative ministry. Catholics tend to weaken the element of the community being represented in ministry. Evangelicals tend to evacuate the Eucharist of something essential: Jesus Christ presiding at his own table. In fact, as we have seen in Aquinas, the idea of the priest/minister representing Christ is by no means incompatible with the idea of the minister/priest representing the people. The Church's ministers act in the name of Christ and on behalf of the whole Church.

The same debate, about who represents whom, was played out in Anglican theology in the nineteenth century. The background was the Tractarians' reaffirmation of apostolic authority, which in turn provoked a low-church reaction. F. D. Maurice sought a way through this kind of polarizing of theologies. He attacked the low-church reductionist fallacy that if something is true of Christ himself it cannot also be true of his Church: if Christ is Priest there cannot be a human priesthood. The reverse is the case, he argues: only Christ's priesthood makes a human priesthood possible. Any office that the Church exercises must be one that first belongs to Christ. The ministry of the Church must be modelled christologically. As Christ is representative of both God and his people, so is the Christian ministry. The priest ministers on behalf of a present Christ to those who are already joined to him in baptism, not on behalf of an absent Christ to those who are cut off from him without priestly mediation (Maurice 1958: II, 125f, 149).

J. B. Lightfoot's famous dissertation on the Christian ministry, appended to his commentary of Philippians, appealed to Maurice's concept of representative ministry in support of what he saw as a non-sacerdotal understanding of priesthood. Priesthood has to do with representation, not mediation – representing God to humanity and humanity to God. The minister or priest represents God to human beings as God's ambassador, charged with the ministry of reconciliation, proclaiming in God's name the offer of forgiveness and, when it is accepted, pronouncing in God's name again the absolution of the penitent. He is also the people's representative before God: 'He is a priest, as the mouthpiece, the delegate of a priestly race. His acts are not his own but the acts of the congregation' (Lightfoot 1898: 181–269, esp. 267–68).

Charles Gore's notable work *The Church and the Ministry* (1886) showed that a high view of the Church as an historical, ordered, confessing community, and of the episcopate as the primary instrument of continuity, order and doctrinal truth, did not necessarily entail the sort of 'sacerdotal' or mediatorial view of the ministry that Maurice and Lightfoot were so concerned about. While Gore defends the term 'priesthood', as applied to the ordained, he equally insists that the whole Church is 'a high priestly race' because 'it lives in the full enjoyment of [Christ's] reconciliation and is the instrument through which the whole world is to be reconciled to God'. Gore is quite clear that the ordained have a representative, not a vicarious role; theirs is a difference of function, not of kind (Gore 1889: 200, 84).

R. C. Moberly politely took Bishop Lightfoot to task for his blustering about 'sacerdotalism'; frankly, it was a bit of an Aunt Sally. A non-mediatorial priesthood does not mean that the priest is merely the 'delegate' of the congregation: that would be to start out on the slippery slope of reductionism. It is a fallacy to think that a high doctrine of the Church as the Spirit-bearing body of Christ requires a low doctrine of her ministry. For Moberly, the Christian ministry is the instrument that represents the Spirit-endowed body, yet is itself so Spirit-endowed that it has the authority and the power to represent the Church 'instrumentally'. That means that Moberly does not accept Lightfoot's view that the ordained or distinct ministry is dispensable. (Here Moberly swings nineteenth-century Anglican theology of ministry back into the historic mainstream, Protestant as well as Catholic.) There is, rather, an organic relation between the body and its ministry.

> The Christian ministry is not a substituted intermediary – still less an atoning mediator – between God and lay people; but it is rather the representative and organ of the whole body, in the exercise of prerogatives and powers which belong to the body as a whole. It is ministerially empowered to wield, as the body's organic representative, the powers which belong to the body, but which the body cannot wield except through its own organs, duly fitted for the purpose. (Moberly 1969: 241–42)

'Christ or the Church?' is surely a false dichotomy. Christ cannot be separated from his Body. The ministry of the Church necessarily represents both Christ and the Church (or as we could say, Christ-in-the-Church). Ministry consists of public actions, owned by the Christian community, that witness to and manifest the nature and life of the community as the body of Christ, in and through which he is at work, in and through which his presence becomes known. Ministers represent him not in the vicarious sense that they take the place of an absent Christ, but in the realist sense that they are instruments or agents that make Christ truly present, not primarily through any personal sanctity that they may possess, but precisely through the means of grace that he has provided. The concept of representation avoids the twin pitfalls of ministerial theology: either identifying the ordained with Christ himself, to the detriment of the laity, or separating Christ from his body, in ecclesiological reductionism, on the other.

It provides for some critical distance between the ordained ministry and Christ. It neither divinizes the ordained ministry nor empties it of its God-given significance.

Because the Church's ministry is representative it has the nature of a sign: there is a sense in which it is sacramental. It is an outward, visible sign of a spiritual reality – a reality located not so much in the interior life of the ordained, as in the calling of the Church and the means of grace that are given to enable her to be worthy of her calling. The ministry of the God-given means of grace (principally word and sacrament) shows forth, though always inadequately and not without distortion, the true nature of the Church as Christ's body. A dedicated ministry, serving the means of grace, can mirror God in the performance of its tasks – but only 'in a glass darkly' (1 Corinthians 13.12). What the ministry does is to lead the way in doing what the Church must do and acting as the Church must act. It is always what A. T. Hanson called 'the pioneer ministry' (Hanson 1961: 155), revealing and serving something greater than itself.

An apostolic ministry in an apostolic community

The Apostles were the pioneer ministers *par excellence*: their witness is the benchmark for the authenticity of the Church's message in subsequent ages. Unless it is apostolic the Church is not authentic. The apostolicity of the Church links past and present in its mission: it connects its ground and origin, on the one hand, and its ongoing life and ministry, on the other. To put it another way, the apostolicity of the Church refers to its mission, to the fulfilment of the tasks entrusted to it by Christ. An apostle is a person 'sent forth', not merely as a messenger, but as a delegate of the one who sends, bearing his authority (Lightfoot 1905: 92). Mark calls the disciples Apostles when they return from their mission of proclaiming, healing and exorcizing (Mark 6.30). The apostolate is not limited to the Twelve, nor is it restricted to the larger company reckoned as apostles in the New Testament: it embraces all Christians. In the second half of the twentieth century, the Roman Catholic Church began to speak the language of 'the apostolate of the laity'. The calling of every Christian is twofold: to discipleship and to apostleship.

In the New Testament this mission, these tasks, are given to the Apostles, but it is clear that they are given to them precisely as representatives of the whole Church. They are not only the unique witnesses of the risen Lord, but also the Church in embryo, in microcosm. That twofold relation of the Apostles to the Church is clear in the interchangeable way that the New Testament refers to them and to the whole community.

- In Matthew 28.16 we find the Great Commission being given only to the eleven disciples.
- In the longer ending of Mark the command to go into all the world and proclaim the gospel to the whole creation is likewise given to the eleven (Mark 16.14).
- In Luke, however, the eleven who are to proclaim repentance and forgiveness to all nations are accompanied by the rest of the assembled disciples (Luke 24.33).
- The Acts of the Apostles refers to this group as the Apostles, but links with them a group of women, including Mary the Mother of Jesus, and with his brothers (Acts 1.13–14).
- In John 20 the risen Lord appears to a group that is described indiscriminately as 'the disciples' or 'the Twelve', sends them forth, breathes his Spirit upon them and gives them authority to remit or retain sins.
- In the High Priestly Prayer of John 17, on the other hand, Jesus prays both for those who have believed and those who will come to believe through their word. He makes no difference between them in what he prays for them. They are all to be one, they are all to be consecrated by the word of truth, they are all sent into

the world as the Father has sent Jesus into the world. They are all 'apostled'.

To sum up this biblical material: in the New Testament we find a distinct band of Apostles set in the midst of a wider group of disciples. As Wingren pointed out, in the New Testament the ministry of word and sacrament is given only to the Apostles, but is actually performed by many.

> In the New Testament there is not a single line which speaks of a commission given by Christ to preach the gospel to the nations which does not also refer to the person sent out *eo ipso* an apostle. The charge given by Christ to preach the gospel is quite clearly an apostolic commission ... According to the New Testament, baptism, the preaching of the gospel, and the eucharist ... have been entrusted ... only to the apostles, but ... all of them are administered by persons other than apostles, though the New Testament does not tell us how these functions passed from the apostles. (Wingren 1964: 126–7)

In their commentary on the Fourth Gospel, Hoskyns and Davey made a similar point:

> The controversy whether the commission is given to the Church as a whole or to the apostles is irrelevant. There is no distinction here between the Church and the ministry; both completely overlap. The evangelist records the birth of the Church as the organism of the spirit of God, and the origin of the authority of the ministry. Both are inaugurated together ... The Christian community was, at its inception, a community of Apostles. (Hoskyns and Davey 1947: 545–6)

Thus the Apostles are identified with the Church as a whole in two ways: in the commission to ministry and in the bestowal of the Spirit. In the persons of the Apostles the whole Church is commissioned to exercise a ministry. Its mission takes the form of a ministry involving preaching, baptizing and discipling. In the persons of the Apostles the whole Church receives the gift of the Holy Spirit precisely to empower it to carry out that mission and ministry. What we have in the New Testament is not a ministry that is the exclusive bearer of apostolicity, set in relation to a community that lacks it and depends entirely on the ministry for it, but an apostolic ministry set within an equally apostolic community.

The Church of England's Doctrine Commission of 1922–1938 grasped this fact about the ministry's relation to the Church. The Acts of the Apostles, their report pointed out, presents the Church on the day of Pentecost as 'a body of believers having within it, as its recognised focus of unity and organ of authority, the Apostolate, which owed its origin to the action of the Lord himself.' The Commission continued:

> There was not first an Apostolate which gathered a body of believers about itself; nor was there a completely structureless collection of believers which gave authority to the apostles to speak and act on its behalf ... From the first there was the fellowship of believers finding its unity in the Twelve. (Doctrine Commission 1938: 114–15)

The 1967 Synod of Bishops of the Roman Catholic Church also spoke of the inseparability of the Apostles and the Church: 'It is clear from the New Testament writings that an apostle and a community of faithful united with one another by a mutual link under Christ as head and the influence of his Spirit belong to the original inalienable structure of the Church' (Flannery 1982: 678). From the principle of the inseparability of the Apostles and the Church – indeed, the virtual interchangeability of the two in several New Testament texts – we can draw two conclusions:

First, the Apostles represent the Church, so that what is said of the Apostles – that they are sent forth in the name of Christ, that they are given authority to pronounce the forgiveness of sins, and that they are endued with the Spirit – must be predicated of the Church as a whole. It is the Church as such that is given these gifts. The Church is apostolic in its essential nature.

Second, there is a distinction to be drawn between the Church as a whole – the entire body of believers – and those who exercise a distinctive ministry within and on behalf of that body. Although the whole Church is apostolic, Apostle and Church are not fully interchangeable. As *Baptism, Eucharist and Ministry* says: 'The Church has never been without persons holding specific authority and responsibility' (BEM 1982: 21 [M9]). Within a fully apostolic community we have a distinct apostolic ministry.

So we find ourselves confronted with a paradox and having to hold two principles in tension. On the one hand, Christ's commission and his gift of the power of the Spirit are given to the whole Church. On the other hand, there is an apostolic ministry with distinct authority and responsibility that is not exercised by all. These two points are not really in conflict. In fact they are two fundamental axioms of a theology of ministry. They need each other. The one cannot stand without the other, and this is for two reasons:

• Unless the commission and the gift of the Spirit were given to the whole Church, the Apostles and their successors would be detached from the community of early disciples which included the women and Jesus's brothers, with the result that the ordained ministry that succeeded them thereafter would be isolated from the body of Christ. This would mean an apostolic ministry ministering to a non-apostolic community. In other words, there could be no representative ministry, because the distinctive ministry would not be embodying, focusing and reflecting back the nature of the Church.

• But, on the other hand, if there were no distinct authoritative ministry, stemming from the Apostles, the whole body could not be called to realize its nature as apostolic. How else can the Church be enabled to realize its apostolic nature if not through a distinct ministry that calls the Church, from a position of recognized authority, to become what it is by focusing, reflecting and emboding that apostolicity for the benefit of the whole body?

The Synod of Roman Catholic Bishops in 1967 deduced from the kind of New Testament evidence that I have set out that the essential structure of the Church, that of the flock and its pastors, remains the norm (Flannery 1982: 679). It is not easy to simultaneously affirm the two principles that we have identified – that of the apostolic community and that of the apostolic ministry. The attempt to do so has given rise to some contorted theology which cannot quite bring itself to say that the priesthood of all the baptized and the ordained priesthood are, or are not, of the same order of the gifts of grace (see the discussion in Avis 1990: ch. 6). However, the two can be reconciled and integrated in the idea of a representative ministry.

Responsibility for the ministry of word and sacrament and for pastoral oversight, is given not purely to the ordained ministry, but in the first place and fundamentally to the Church as such, to the whole Church, or to the Church generally, as part of its commission as the apostolic community. This triple mandate is necessarily accompanied by the gift of the Spirit, because the whole Church is mandated to make disciples of all nations and can only attempt this in the power of the Spirit (Luke 24.46–49; Acts 1.8). The Church makes provision for pastoral oversight when it makes provision for an ordained ministry and provides the resources for it. The ministry of the word, of the sacraments and of pastoral oversight is exercised, not by every member, but by a distinct ordained ministry, through which the Church as a whole exercises the ministry that belongs to its nature.

If the mission of the Church and the gift of the Spirit are given to the whole Church, yet exercised in public authoritative ways through an ordained ministry, the latter must be said to represent the former. Our argument pivots on the principle of representativeness. The issue of representativeness lies at the heart of apostolicity. It manifests the principle of transmitted authority. The Father sends the Son to speak and act on his behalf. The Son sends the Spirit as 'another Paraclete'. In the power of the Spirit the Son sends his Apostles into the world. But they lead the way in doing what the whole Church in every member is sent to do. The fundamental principle is expressed in Jesus's words, 'To receive you is to receive me, and to receive me is to receive the one who sent me' (Matthew 10.40) and 'Whoever listens to you listens to me' (Luke 10.16). The Apostles are 'ambassadors (*presbeuomen*) for Christ' (2 Corinthians 5.20) so that every Christian in his or her daily life may be Christ's ambassador. All baptized believers live, speak and act for Christ. United with him in baptism, a Christian is *in persona Christi*. In representing Christ, Christians at the same time represent the Church, his body (*in persona ecclesiae*).

Patterns of representation

Our case for representative ministry needs to take on board the evident fact that there are degrees of representativeness. For a start, ordained ministers represent Christ and the Church in a particular way compared with lay Christians. They are given authority to speak and act in public, rather than simply private ways. Those lay people who have a recognized, commissioned ministry share in this strong form of representativeness. There is nothing unevangelical or unreformed in accepting this. The Anglican–Reformed dialogue says:

> The minister as leader has a representative character, to act as 'the one on behalf of the many', so that the whole Church is represented in his person as he carries on his heart the concerns of all his people. He does not act in his own name, but in the name of Christ, and in the name of the whole body of Christ, so that he is at once the

mouthpiece of our Lord and the mouthpiece of his flock. (GROU, para. 85)

However, even within the ordained ministry of the Church, there are degrees of representativeness. Some have a wider sphere of ministry than others and relate to larger communities. While some ordained ministers operate within the sphere of a single benefice, circuit or congregation, others operate within a diocese, a district or a province. This is perhaps another way of looking at the threefold form of ordained ministry delineated by *Baptism, Eucharist and Ministry*: communal, collegial and personal.

- *Communal.* The whole body, the apostolic community, the royal priesthood of the baptized, represents Christ and the Church. It expresses this representative ministry particularly through the conciliar structures of the Church, with its synods, assemblies and conferences. Every Christian shares in the responsibility for the mission, worship and doctrine of the Church.
- *Collegial.* Collegiality has a narrower and a broader sense. In its narrower sense, developed at the Second Vatican Council and adapted by other episcopal Churches – though obviously without the element of 'hierarchical communion' with the Pope – collegiality refers to the collective ministry of bishops as a body and to their relationship with those (mainly presbyters) with whom they share their ministry. In the broader sense, collegiality refers to the way that teams of ministers, ordained and lay, share responsibility and work collaboratively. In both senses, those engaged in a collegial form of ministry represent Christ and the Church, corporately conceived.
- *Personal.* Individuals who are called to special pastoral responsibilities in leadership are awarded a certain prominence. By virtue of their significant profile they represent Christ and the Church at various levels, from

the priest in the parish and the minister in the circuit to the dean in the cathedral, the moderator in the district, the bishop in the diocese, the president in the conference and the archbishop in the province.

Now each tradition, if it finds the communal, collegial and personal typology helpful, must ask itself whether it has a balanced and complete representative ministry. As the official 'Commentary' on the text of *Baptism, Eucharist and Ministry* says:

> These three aspects need to be kept together. In various churches, one or another has been over-emphasised at the expense of the others. In some churches, the personal dimension of the ordained ministry tends to diminish the collegial and communal dimensions. In other churches, the collegial or communal dimension takes so much importance that the ordained ministry loses its personal dimension. Each church needs to ask itself in what way its exercise of the ordained ministry has suffered in the course of history. (BEM 1982: M26)

Ecumenical dialogue can help Churches to see themselves more honestly and to learn from each other's strengths and weaknesses. Anglicans, if I may say so, seem to be quite strong on the communal (with church government being carried out through elected, representative structures from the parish, through deanery and diocesan synods to the General Synod). Anglicans also emphasize the personal: the pastoral leadership of the bishop in the diocese and of the incumbent in the parish are salient features of Anglicanism. But Anglicans are comparatively weak on the collegial dimension and are beginning to address this lack. In the Church of England much thought and effort is being devoted to Local Ministry Teams of ordained and lay ministers in the parishes. Cathedrals have been undergoing reform to provide greater collegiality between the dean, the residentiary canons, the prebendaries and the lay representatives of the cathedral congregation and even the wider community served by the cathedral in the city and county.

The House of Bishops of the Church of England has been reflecting recently on how it might develop the collegial aspect of its own work (see House of Bishops 2000).

Where can Anglicans look for a theology of collegiality? The concept has become identified with Roman Catholic ecclesiology (where it was developed in the teaching of the Second Vatican Council). The Roman Catholic model is structured by the principle of 'hierarchical communion' with the Pope, entailing an obedience that is underpinned by a juridical system. There is nothing comparable to this in Anglicanism. In Anglicanism, communion between the thirty-eight provinces is primarily fraternal and the authority of the bishops gathered at the Lambeth Conference is a moral not a juridical or binding authority. The integrity of each diocese as the local Church is safeguarded. The member Churches of the Communion are legally autonomous but spiritually and pastorally interdependent. The bishops of a province or national Church work collegially within the framework of a common liturgy, canon law and policy on ministry. But these are decided not by the bishops alone but by the synodical governing body of the Church.

The Protestant Churches, on the other hand, are perhaps strong on the communal and collegial aspects of representative ministry, with their structured forms of lay participation and their fundamental parity of ministers (expressed, for example, in the Methodist connexional system and Conference and in the Reformed tradition's synods or courts at various levels. But are these Churches equally strong on the personal form of representative ministry? There are indications that the Protestant Churches are currently engaging in some heart-searching on this score. There seems to be a growing recognition that *episkope* needs a human face. Above all, perhaps, leadership in mission requires a personal focus. The Protestant tradition has generally emphasized the 'parity of ministers' and the singleness of ordained ministry and in so far as this points to genuine collegiality and the corporate responsibility of the ordained it is salutary. But when the demands of mission are foremost, personal *episkope* comes into its own. In the Church of England's ordinal in the *Alternative Service Book 1980* bishops are called to lead the Church in mission. As we shall see immediately, the demands of mission must be allowed to shape the threefold ministry.

In concluding this section, we need to be absolutely clear that all Churches have a ministry of *episkope* and that in all of them it takes communal, collegial and personal forms. Otherwise they would not be Churches of Christ. They all recognize a distribution of gifts, a variety of callings, a sharing of responsibility – in other words, some sense of holy order. All major traditions have a representative ministry. But the emphasis and balance within this economy of representation varies and there is development going on. All have their strengths and weaknesses. During the past century Anglicans have strengthened the communal dimension, by taking the principle of representative government into their system in the form of synodical structures, and they are now giving urgent attention to the collegial dimension. On the other hand, some of the Free Churches are evidently beginning to ask themselves how they can strengthen the personal dimension of *episkope* without undermining their communal and collegial principles. The working out of personal *episkope* is a sensitive issue for the Protestant Churches which have an understandable aversion to hierarchy. However, the personal focus of leadership is indispensable to the life and mission of the Church. As the Swedish Lutheran–Roman Catholic Dialogue report *The Office of Bishop* (1993) insists, personal *episkope* is vital because the Christian Church 'does not know of any impersonal structures or any kind of power apparatus'. That report further emphasizes this point when it states: 'The duty to be a shepherd cannot, therefore, be replaced with impersonal structures from which personal authority, personal responsibility and, on principle, possible martyrdom are absent' (*The Office of Bishop* 1993: 81, 83).

3

ORDAINED TO A MINISTRY SHAPED BY MISSION

Holy Order

In *The City of God* St Augustine devotes the nineteenth book to an enquiry into the supreme good for humankind. With the civilized world crumbling around him under the barbarian onslaught, Augustine evokes a vision of tranquil stability. The good is found when peace and harmony reign in every area of life: in body and mind, between humans in the home and in the city, between nations and between humans and God. The instinctive aim of all creatures is peace and peace is the result of order: 'the peace of the whole universe is the tranquillity of order – and order is the arrangement of things equal and unequal in a pattern which assigns to each its proper position' (Augustine 1972: 870). There is a proper ordering of the Church's life and ministry also (see further Wood 2000).

All Christians are called to a life of discipleship and apostleship, to represent Christ, to speak and act in his name. Clergy and laity are united in a common calling, a partnership with one another and with Christ (Hebrews 3.1, 14) that transcends the distinction between lay and ordained. The people of God, the *laos*, includes both ordained and not ordained (1 Peter 2). Both are embraced within the royal prophetic priesthood. Lay and ordained share in the common task according to the Spirit's distribution of gifts to the Church. However, there are undoubtedly differences in the calling of Christians and there are particular ways in which various lay and ordained vocations represent Christ. The Holy Spirit bestows on the community diverse and complementary gifts for the common good (BEM 1982: M5). The representativeness of lay and ordained is interdependent and must be held together. Our common calling counteracts the inveterate insidious tendency towards ecclesiastical elitism.

There is, so to speak, an economy in what St Paul calls the distributions or apportionings (*diaireseis*: 1 Corinthians 12.4) of gifts and ministries. The ancient Greek patristic concept of economy (*oikonomia*) implies that there is a God-given purpose governing and regulating the life of the Church and that, in order to promote that purpose, there is a particular distribution of gifts, tasks, responsibilities and the authority to fulfil them. Economy suggests restraint, discipline and the various distribution of responsibilities – in other words, holy order. By virtue of holy order, a pattern of ministry is appointed in the Church. The Roman Catholic, Eastern and Oriental Orthodox, Anglican, Old Catholic and some Lutheran Churches adhere to the threefold ministry of bishops, priests and deacons, ordained in historical succession. The non-episcopal Protestant Churches have their own distribution of representative ministries in which the principle of holy order is respected within a greater equality of ministries.

It is an apostolic imperative that, in the worship and ministry of the Church, 'all things should be done decently and in order' (1 Corinthians 14.40); or as Thiselton (2000: 1167–8) translates it: 'fittingly and in an ordered manner'. The idea of holy order stems from this Pauline use. It became clericalized in medieval times and was used to refer to the clerical body as a whole or to one group within it (e.g. *ordo episcopatus*: Power 1969: 62–4). The schoolmen, such as St Thomas Aquinas and St Bonaventure, grounded the doctrine of holy order in a theology of the order and beauty of the divine nature. St Thomas builds on the axiom that the works of God in the created order (*opera ad extra*) reflect the being of God: there is an analogy of being (*analogia entis*) between the Creator and the creation. God's created works must, therefore, reflect God's own order and beauty. The Church has been brought into being by God and must, therefore, like the rest of the creation, exhibit the orderly beauty of God.

> Consequently, in order that this beauty might not be lacking in the Church, God established order in it, in such a way that certain persons minister the sacraments to others, and in this way they are similar to God, as it were, working along with God. (Aquinas, *Summa Theologiae*, *Suppl.*, xxxiv, a, 1, *Resp.*; cited Osborne 1988: 212–13, slightly altered)

For St Thomas and the medievals this beauty and order took a hierarchical form: everything in creation – invisible and visible, angels, humans, and non-human animate creatures – had its appointed place in the great chain of being which included social distinctions based on deference and obedience to higher authority. A good deal of this still clings to the Roman Catholic Church's teaching about holy order and collateral matters: the authority of the magisterium, the exclusion of women from the ordained ministry and the exclusion of lay people from church government. To modern eyes, the rigidly hierarchical structure of holy order, with its connotations of social deference, economic disadvantage and political oppression, seems far from beautiful or admirable. It strikes many people today as unjust and therefore repellent: the important truths of order and authority are obscured for them by historical distortions.

However, unchallengeable hierarchy, social stratification and a caste-like exclusiveness are not intrinsic to holy order. An egalitarian, socially holistic interpretation is equally possible. An interesting attempt has been made to rehabilitate the idea of hierarchy as 'subordination without inequality' (Horne in Hall and Hannaford, eds 1996: 1–19, especially 15). In this spirit I take the expression 'holy order' to mean essentially that there is a diversity of gifts and callings and a distribution of responsibilities – an 'economy' (*oikonomia*) – in ministry and that this is recognized in a 'sacramental' way. Holy order signifies that there is a distinction within the one body between the whole apostolic community of the baptized and those within that community who are commissioned to exercise a public, representative ministry. The idea is captured in Colossians 1.25 which has Paul say, 'I became a minister (*diakonos*) of the Church according to the economy of God (*oikonomian tou theou*) that was given to me for you.'

Holy order does not mean that the ordained are holy and the unordained are not, or even that the ordained are more holy in their lives than the unordained. The ordering is of the whole Church. The ordering is holy because it is God's ordering and because the Church is ordered to the worship and service of God. And even though we sometimes – not improperly – speak of the three orders of bishop, priest and deacon, there is in truth a single holy order in the Church – and there is a sense in which it includes those baptized persons who are not ordained.

The fact that lay people, as well as clergy, are ordered to their particular vocation through baptism has led some to propose that there is an 'order' of laity, in the same way that deacons, presbyters and bishops each comprise an order (Zizioulas 1985: 152–3). This approach is reflected in the 1979 *Book of Common Prayer* of the Episcopal Church of the USA ('Concerning the Service of the Church', p. 13; see also Miller, 2002). However, what some have seen as the ordination, so to speak, of the laity through baptism is actually the ordination of the *laos*, of the whole people of God and does not distinguish clergy from laity in the sense of the not-ordained. We do not need to posit a separate 'order of laity' when we say that baptism effects 'as it were, the ordination of a new member of the royal priesthood' (Richardson 1958: 301). Nevertheless, 'lay people', as members of the *laos*, are 'ordered' to their role and ministry in the Church, as sharers in Christ's prophetic, priestly and royal anointing.

Holy order establishes the particular ministries of bishops, presbyters and deacons and of lay people. These ministries are ordered in relation to the Church as a body and in relation to each other. Holy order creates interdependent forms of ministry that are mutually constitutive (as we shall see below). In particular, without the ordering of lay people, holy order applied to the ordained would be meaningless. It is the ordering of the whole Church that makes it possible for ministry to take communal, collegial and personal forms. In episcopally ordered Churches, however, where the personal dimension of *episkope* is fully recognized, the bishop's ministry may be regarded as the linchpin of holy order, since the bishop of the diocese is responsible for the selection, training, ordination, licensing and oversight of clergy and for the oversight of comparable processes for recognized lay ministers within the framework of the Church's canon law.

Though common to all baptized believers in varying degrees, the principle of representation is seen most clearly in the ordained ministry, which is properly called a representative ministry (as we have seen earlier). Even there it finds expression in different ways according to the divine economy, with the office of bishop being undoubtedly the fullest expression of representativeness. Episcopal ministry represents the Church in a wider sphere than other clergy and ministers, holding together Christian communities in space and time. Bishops are ordained by other bishops in a communion that spreads through Christian history and the Christian *oikumene*. The representative nature of the bishop's ministry across time is expressed through the succession of the ordinations they perform, with the laying on of hands by the bishop, together with presbyters. It is also expressed in the tangible continuity of the bishop's ministry of word, sacrament and pastoral oversight in an historic see (the seat of the bishop within a diocese, from which the diocese often takes its name: e.g. Canterbury, York, London). The issue of visible continuity through history brings us to the principle of transmitted authority in particular.

At its most basic, the principle of transmitted authority, which is common to all mainstream Churches in one form or another, safeguards the decency and good order in the Church that St Paul called for. It is intended to prevent individuals seizing office for themselves or capturing a factional following. But it also ensures continuity and authenticity in the ministry of word and sacrament and is therefore one of the ways in which the apostolicity of the Church – its faithfulness in mission to its origin and foundation – is expressed and secured. As Moberly put it, it is 'the principle that ministerial office is an outward and orderly institution, dependent for its validity upon transmission, continuous and authorized, from the Apostles, whose own commission was direct from Jesus Christ' (Moberly 1969: 115).

Continuity of ministerial authority should surely be expressed in communal, collegial and personal modes. For episcopally ordered Churches, the succession of bishops in office and in their local Churches (sees) is a salient expression of continuity and transmitted authority in the personal mode. In episcopal Churches, the bishop is the pivot of transmitted authority for ministry. In reformed episcopal polities, such as that of Anglicanism, for example, the bishop's role in the transmission of authority is both supported and constrained by synodical government which sets the framework of canon law, under which the bishop operates, and also provides the resources for the ministry and mission of the Church.

Representing Christ and the Church

All the baptized may be called to a representative ministry. As I have explained, I take ministry, properly speaking, to be the service of God in the cause of the Kingdom which is recognized by the Church. It is not the purely personal witness that Christians bear to Christ in their daily discipleship, but has a public dimension in which, in some sense, it is mandated by and 'stands for' the Church as a body. Recent theology of ministry (O'Meara 1983; Collins 1990, 1992, 2002) has stressed that there is an element of commissioning and therefore of authority in all ministry. Ministry is a task carried out on behalf of the body which is recognized by the body.

There is, of course, a private and individual aspect to this. Through faith and baptism Christians are united with Christ. Their Christ-centred identity means that all Christians, when living out their calling, represent Christ to others. All represent Christ and his Church by virtue of their baptism which has united them to Christ in his death and resurrection. All the baptized, as private individuals, embody the principle *in persona Christi* in an informal way. They carry Christ in their hearts and witness to him in their lives. The momentum of Christian spirituality and mission stems from the fact that the baptized live, speak and act for Christ. They are individually members of his body and temples of the Holy Spirit (1 Corinthians 6.19).

But we are concerned primarily with the public and representative aspect of service. Within the calling of the whole Church to represent Christ, lay people who have a recognized ministry of the word, who assist with the ministry of the sacraments and in pastoral responsibility have a notable representative function as they are called to speak and act on behalf of the Church. In the Church of England, for example, these are readers, churchwardens, evangelists, pastoral assistants, Parochial Church Council members and elected members of houses of laity in synodical bodies. In the Protestant Churches these include elders (though, in the Reformed tradition, elders are actually regarded as ordained), deacons and stewards. These lay people represent Christ-in-his-body to others, whether fellow Christians in the Church or non-Christian neighbours in the world.

The principle of representativeness can be seen even more clearly, I suggest, in the ministry of the ordained, for within the body of Christ there are ministries that are given authority to speak and act in a public way that goes beyond what lay people are authorized to do. The ordained are called, trained, commissioned, licensed and accountable to authority in a particular way. Through the ministry of word and sacrament and the exercise of pastoral oversight they carry out a public ministry of Christ in the congregation and in the local community. Though all the baptized share in Christ's threefold messianic office as prophet, priest and king, individuals may not take it upon themselves to claim a public ministry for themselves in which they speak and act on behalf of all. As Luther for one insisted, invoking a time-honoured principle, what is given to the whole body no private individual may arrogate to himself without the authority of the body. Similarly, the Thirty-Nine Articles lay down that 'It is not lawful for any man to take upon him the office of publick preaching, or ministering the Sacraments in the Congregation, before he be lawfully called, and sent to execute the same ... by men who have publick authority given unto them' (Article XXIII).

Lay ministry

There is only one mission, that of Jesus Christ through his body the Church (1 Corinthians 12.12). The universal mission must consist primarily in discharging the original commission given to the Apostles (here standing for the Church) by the risen Christ. That commission comprises the

2).

tasks or mandated activities of the Church. The Great Commission of Matthew 28.18–20 refers to three tasks: teaching (i.e. the ministry of the word), baptizing (i.e. the ministry of the sacraments) and making disciples (i.e. the ministry of pastoral oversight). Clearly these are tasks that the ordained occupy themselves with. But are they also given to lay people? Let us consider them one at a time.

The ministry of the word is clearly not confined to clergy and ministers. Some lay people, such as Anglican readers and Methodist lay preachers, are called, trained and commissioned to minister the word and they perform this ministry on behalf of Christ and the Church (*in persona Christi* and *in persona ecclesiae*). Some lay people thus share with the clergy and ministers in a representative ministry of the word, though they minister as assistants to those who have pastoral oversight, 'the cure of souls'.

To what extent may lay people have a representative sacramental ministry? There is a long-standing tradition that, in a pastoral emergency, lay people may baptize. Luther invokes the practice of baptism by midwives in support of his doctrine of the universal priesthood of baptized Christians. There is nothing greater than baptism, he claims. If a lay person can baptize, they can, in principle, do anything. The Reformed tradition was not hospitable to this practice. Calvin frowned on it and the Westminster Confession does not permit it (XXVII, iv). But this may be regarded as the exception that proves the rule. Laity also assist at the Eucharist, though in most traditions they do not preside, for presidency at the Eucharist normally belongs to those to whom pastoral oversight of the community (including the ministry of the word) is entrusted (cf. House of Bishops, *Eucharistic Presidency*, 1997). But lay people are certainly involved, not only in the ministry of the word at the Eucharist and in leading the intercessions, but at the offertory, serving at the altar, administering the cup and in liturgical processions. However, this lay ministry of the sacraments takes the form of assisting the president who has or shares oversight.

While it would be generally acknowledged that lay people play a part in the ministry of the word and also assist in the administration of the sacraments, it is perhaps not so clear whether laity may also have a representative ministry of pastoral responsibility in the form of care and oversight. Clearly all Christians are called to show pastoral care to one another and to their non-Christian neighbours: 'Bear one another's burdens and so fulfil the law of Christ' (Galatians 6.2). This is not an optional extra, but a responsibility that can never be taken away. It is the inalienable calling of Christians to emulate the Good Shepherd (John 10.11ff.; 21.15ff.). The faithful must never be discouraged or disempowered from doing this. The service for the ordination of a bishop in the Church of England's *Alternative Service Book 1980* recognizes that the bishop is called to work with the people of God in the oversight of the Church. Pastoral oversight is a charge that is given generally to the Church as a community or society.

However, it would not make sense to say that every individual Christian has the sort of pastoral responsibility whereby they are given authority to 'oversee' their fellow Christians. There is a distinct ministry of pastoral oversight (*episkope*) within the Church which goes beyond the pastoral care that all Christians should have for one another. This kind of oversight is not, however, entirely confined to the clergy: there are recognized lay ministries that individually or collectively involve some degree of oversight, such as churchwardens, members of Parochial Church Councils and of the houses of laity in synodical bodies, stewards and members of Methodist synods and of Conference. There are equivalents to most of these in other Churches; the Roman Catholic Church is second to none in using lay people in liturgical and pastoral roles (though not formally in church government). The Roman Catholic Code of Canon Law

(1983) makes provision for the bishop, with the permission of the Holy See, to delegate or depute pastoral charge of parishes, preaching, baptisms and marriages to lay people (Canons 517:2 and 1112). Anglicanism, for its part, recognizes the responsibility of the laity in church government and gives lay people a formal role in the discernment of doctrine through houses of laity in synodical government (though at least as far as the Church of England is concerned, not the *proposal* of doctrine). Thus in Methodism and in Anglicanism the laity have a constitutional role in consultation, discernment and decision making on behalf of the Church. As far as pastoral *oversight* is concerned, however, lay ministers do no more – but no less – than assist and advise those who are entrusted with *episkope*: the diocesan bishop assisted by and working collaboratively with the presbyterate.

Ordained ministry

Pre-accupation with 'authoriy'!!

By looking at the ministry of laity, deacons, priests and bishops, we can see that the principle of representativeness is related to the principle of authority for public ministry. I prefer to envisage this not in a hierarchical sense, like a pyramid, with all the energy flowing from the top downwards, but as a pattern or constellation of distinctive ministries all of which have equal validity and value. However, while all acknowledged ministries have their own integrity, there are differences of scope that are related to the authority that is given. It would serve no good purpose to pretend, for reasons of political correctness, that this is not the case! In all Churches there are differences in the authority that is awarded and this is somehow related to the scope or range of ministries that are authorized.

- A lay minister, such as a reader, local preacher, lay parish assistant or pastoral auxiliary, churchwarden, or their equivalents in various traditions, is given authority by Christ in his Church for certain tasks which may include the ministry of the word, assisting with the sacraments and ministering pastoral care, mostly in local and circumscribed situations.

- A deacon is given authority by Christ in his Church to carry out certain forms of ministry (caring for people pastorally; assisting in leading worship; teaching and preaching; administering Communion; baptizing in the absence of the priest or at the request of the priest; officiating at marriages; above all helping to bring the needs of the world and the means of grace in the Church together). A deacon has a representative, assisting and non-presidential ministry of word, sacrament and pastoral care.
- A presbyter, while remaining also a deacon (on this point, see below), is given further authority by Christ in his Church to carry out some forms of ministry that are not open to a deacon (presiding at the Eucharist; pronouncing the absolution; giving the blessing; normally holding the cure of souls in a parish; taking part with the bishop in the ordination of presbyters).
- A bishop, while remaining also a deacon and presbyter, is given yet further authority by Christ in his Church to carry out some forms of ministry that are not open to either a deacon or a priest (to confirm; to ordain deacons, priests and other bishops; to exercise oversight of clergy and laity; to preside at the synod of the local Church).

Thus a lay person represents Christ in his body in a range of ministries. A deacon represents Christ in his body in a wider sphere of representation than a lay person does. A presbyter represents Christ in his body in a wider sphere of representation than a deacon does, and a bishop represents Christ in his body in a wider sphere of representation than a priest does. Lay ministry and the three orders of ordained ministry bring to light, in a publicly witnessed way, a progressively wider representation of Christ in his Church, through the ministry of word, sacrament and pastoral oversight. (It is possible to reverse this sequence and to show that presbyters, deacons and lay ministers share in the total ministry of the bishop to varying degrees: this would be a modern Roman Catholic approach, following Vatican II, and would find favour with some Anglicans.)

It is these ministries, carried out with the authority that Christ bestows through the Church in the threefold order, rather than the private persons of bishops, priests and deacons, that effectively represent Christ to the Church and the world. It is not that the person of the ordained minister, as a private individual, represents Christ, as a unique icon of Christ, but that Christ is present in the appointed means of grace ministered by that person with the authority and charisma bestowed in ordination. The only ministry of the Church – of laity and clergy – is the ministry of Jesus Christ himself. That is why, though the Church rightly expects the character and demeanour of the minister and his or her lifestyle to reflect something of the nature and character of God, the Church insists that the unworthiness of the minister does not destroy the efficacy of the means of grace (Article XXVI). But within the economy of holy order there are various callings through which Christ ministers to his body and through his body to the world.

The principle of representativeness, properly understood and safeguarded, is vital because it insists that the risen Christ works through unworthy human instruments to minister his grace and presence for the salvation of the world. With the authority that comes from Christ in his body, these appointed ministries of word, sacrament and pastoral oversight represent Christ in ways that he has ordained within the economy of the one *missio dei*. The diversity of callings that is distributed in a pattern of holy order is part of God's purpose for the Church. But how are the various callings discerned and how is order preserved?

I have suggested that ministry is properly understood as God-given work for the Kingdom that is acknowledged by the Church. How is it acknowledged? Who does the acknowledging? Of course there are, as we have seen, important informal ways in which a person's gifts come to be acknowledged in a community and much recognition takes place at a purely local level. There is also a need for someone to evaluate that discernment and to declare what has been discerned. What it comes down to is: who gives authority to minister?

In episcopally ordered Churches that role usually belongs to the bishop individually and to the college of bishops corporately (in Methodism it derives from the Conference). They draw on the expertise of national and local advisors in formulating policy and in making judgements about individuals. In episcopally ordered Churches the bishop is the chief pastor of the local Church (the diocese), the one who takes the lead in preaching the gospel, teaching the faith and safeguarding the truth, and the principal minister of the sacraments in that community. A bishop cares for the portion of the people of God committed to his charge: he has the cure (or care) of souls. As well as being directly involved himself in the ministry of word, sacrament and pastoral responsibility, the bishop makes provision for the ministry of word, sacrament and pastoral responsibility throughout his diocese. He does this through those with whom he shares the cure of souls: incumbents and priests in charge of parishes. As Church of England bishops say to the parish priests they institute: the cure of souls is 'both yours and mine'. In episcopally ordered Churches, the parochial ministry is not autonomous. Without the authority of the bishop no one has the ministry of word, sacrament and pastoral care.

The full ministry of the Church is the triple ministry of word, sacrament and pastoral responsibility. Together these make up a whole ministry. They should not be fragmented or divided. Bishops clearly have this ministry and share it with presbyters in pastoral charge. Assistant curates, whether deacons or priests, do not have the cure of souls, but they assist those who do. This is also the situation of permanent deacons: theirs is an assisting ministry (as the Church of England ordinals, for example, make clear) and as such has integrity. Deacons who hope to be priested and priests serving as assistant curates can expect to have that pastoral responsibility themselves in due course. Lay ministers also do not have and never will have the cure of souls, but they assist those who do. Lay ministers, such as readers, have their own distinguished form of ministry. Non-stipendiary ministers may be given the cure of souls as priests in charge (but it is not envisaged that ordained local ministers will ever have the cure of souls; they will not be responsible for parishes; in this respect they are closer to laity or deacons than to other clergy).

It is the birthright of every Christian to enjoy the possibility of having a ministry – a specific form of work for God's Kingdom that is acknowledged by the Church and blessed by the Lord. Another way of speaking about this is representative ministry, one that represents both Christ and the Church. But there are diversities of gifts and callings. Individuals are often not the best judge in their own case. There is a need for public discernment of gifts and callings and public recognition of them by constituted authority. In episcopal Churches this falls to the bishops (in Methodism to the conference; in other Churches to synods), with their special responsibility for doctrine, worship and ministry. Ordained and lay ministers can be called into fellowship with the bishop's ministry, to the extent of sharing in it or assisting in it. Thus we have a bottom-up approach which emphasizes the breadth and freedom of the Spirit's *charismata*, complemented by a top-down approach that stresses duly constituted authority, this also flowing from the Spirit though through different channels.

Within the calling that is common to all Christians – to

live as disciples of Jesus Christ – there are specific callings to lay and ordained representative ministry. One aspect of that, which is not given to lay ministers, deacons or ordained local ministers, is the pastoral charge of a community (the cure of souls within a parish) in fellowship and collegiality with the bishop who is 'the chief pastor of all that are within his diocese, as well laity as clergy, and their father in God' (Church of England: Canon C18).

The diaconate: a flagship ministry

A great debate is currently taking place on the nature of the diaconate. The interpretation of the New Testament word *diakonia* is in a state of ferment as a radically different meaning of this crucial term takes hold. This interpretation has implications for our understanding of Christian ministry, both ordained and lay, and its shaping by the *missio dei*. The discussion is happening both within and between the Churches.

- Among Anglicans there are widespread misgivings about the long-standing tendency to regard the diaconate as merely transitional to ordination to the priesthood and doubts about the traditional emphasis on deacons as humble servants of others. The ministry of 'permanent', 'distinctive' or 'vocational' deacons is being considered with fresh interest in many parts of the Anglican Communion.
- For Roman Catholics Vatican II gave a new impetus to the distinctive diaconate (but without spelling out in any detail how it would work) that is still filtering through to dioceses.
- Lutherans, on the other hand, have a strong tradition of *diakonia* as a pastoral, social and educational ministry on behalf of the Church – though not usually divorced from the ministry of the word.
- In the Methodist Church of Great Britain deacons are

ordained primarily to a pastoral role: any official preaching or sacramental ministry that they may have is incidental, in a sense, to the formal intention of their ordination.

- In the Orthodox Churches deacons may remain deacons for some years but their function is mainly liturgical, including preaching.

- In the Reformed tradition, following Calvin's fourfold ministry (pastors, teachers, elders, deacons), deacons have not generally been ministers of word and sacrament, but their ministry is being re-appraised in some parts of the Reformed Communion (e.g. in the Church of Scotland).

- Among the Moravians, ordination to the diaconate is full ordination to the ministry of word and sacrament – Moravian deacons preside at the Eucharist – while presbyters and bishops are simply 'consecrated'.

Underlying most of these inherited positions is an interpretation of the diaconate as service and of the deacon as a servant of the needy. The standard line makes great play of the fact that a deacon serves and helps those to whom he or she is sent. It sounds very impressive to say that deacons spend themselves in selfless service to the poor, the marginalized and the weak. It is this fundamental assumption that is now being called in question – and no wonder. If service is the defining characteristic of deacons, how does this distinguish them from all lay and ordained Christians and why do they need to be ordained? It is almost as though, in the case of deacons, ordination is a sacramental sign of a morally virtuous disposition, a fruit of the Spirit, humility. That is not what ordination is for. Churches have been agonizing about the diaconate, but their perplexity is created by theologizing on a false premise.

When Greek speakers in the ancient world, whether Christian or not, used *diakonos* and other *diakon-* words they were not generally trying to express a notion of humble service and compassionate care. Their intention was otherwise. To discover this intention and to follow its consequences through our understanding of diaconal and other ministry will lead the Churches out of the impasse.

No one has done more to stimulate the current ferment than John N. Collins, a Roman Catholic layman from Melbourne. His research into the meaning of *diakonia* in classical and New Testament Greek (*Diakonia: Re-interpreting the Ancient Sources*, 1990) is having a seismic effect on the understanding of diaconal ministry. He applied his new insights to the practice of Christian ministry in the provocatively titled *Are All Christians Ministers?* (1992) where he argued that ministry should be distinguished from common Christian discipleship. Discipleship is what all Christians are called to in their baptism. Of course it includes witness and service. But ministry (*diakonia*) is something more. It depends upon a specific divine commission and therefore requires the call or at least the recognition of the Church. Ministry is not something that we can take upon ourselves; it is not the individual's prerogative. If everything is ministry, nothing is.

Recently Collins has returned to the fray with an accessible account of the uses of *diakonia* in the New Testament and in the early Church (Collins 2002). The implications are revolutionary for our thinking about the diaconate. The heart of the argument is that *diakonia* does not mean humble service of the needy. Its connotations are rather of commissioned, responsible agency and authori-tative embassy. Of course, service remains fundamental, but the service involved is primarily the service of the one who sends or commissions, that is, ultimately God. Only secondarily is it service – humble, compassionate service – of those to whom one is sent, who may include the materially needy.

For St Paul, the *diakonia* with which he had been entrusted was a stewardship of God's revelation in Christ, the mystery that had been made known (1 Corinthians 3.5). He and his fellow workers were ministers (*diakonoi*) of a new covenant, not in the accepted usage of 'deacon' that they were *servants* of the covenant, but in the reconstructed sense that the new covenant was the essential content of the authoritative message that they carried from the one who was the mediator of the new covenant. The message of God's reconciliation of the world through Christ constituted Paul and his colleagues as those engaged in the ministry (*diakonia*) of reconciliation (2 Corinthians 3.6; 5.18), the ministry of the word of God, of the gospel of the glory of Christ and of his lordship (2 Corinthians 4.1–5). It was that ministry, one that had Christ as both its source and its content, that caused Paul and his colleagues to consider themselves not servants, but slaves (*douloi*) of the Corinthian Christians (v. 5).

This sense of *diakonos* makes it a close cousin of *apostolos*. St Paul uses both terms of himself almost interchangeably. What links them together is the idea of mission, of being sent forth to fulfil a task on behalf of the one who has the authority to send. It appears to be generally agreed among biblical scholars that *apostolos* is the Greek translation of the Hebrew *shaliach*, a derivative of the verb to send, which in the Septuagint (LXX) is regularly translated by *apostellein*. This was an envoy who represented someone in authority for a particular purpose. In receiving the *shaliach* you received the one who was represented. Incidentally, we are accumulating a cluster of overlapping terms for commissioned, representative ministry: *apostolos*, *presbeutes* (ambassador) and now *diakonos*. Though not synonymous, all three point to the same essential meaning: Christ sends his people in his name to do his work and invests them with his authority.

The Pauline material is crucial for the reconstruction of *diakonia*, but it does not stand alone and unsupported. For Luke too, in the third Gospel and the Acts of the Apostles, *diakonia* was a sacred mandate that had to be carried out. A deacon in ancient usage is one who is commissioned to fulfil a vital task, to carry out a mission on behalf of another, an executive who acts on behalf of a constituted authority. If, guided by Collins, we re-read familiar New Testament texts in this light the results are astonishing.

Mark 10.45 is usually translated: 'The Son of Man came not to be served but to serve and to give his life as a ransom for many.' This breaks the statement into two distinct but connected parts that both refer to the self-giving of Jesus for the sake of the world. The sense of the standard interpretation is that the culmination of Jesus's service to humankind was laying down his life for their sake. Of course this sentiment remains gloriously true, but it may not get the emphasis of the text right. Mark was not making a point about Jesus's inner humility and his motivation to be at the disposal of others. He was emphasizing the authority that lay behind his task and the specific purpose for which God had sent him into the world.

Reinterpreted in the light of fresh research, the text looks rather different and runs something like this: 'The Son of Man came not to give orders, to be waited on and to have people running errands on his behalf, but rather to carry out the mission God has given him, which is to give his life as a ransom for many.' The *diakonia* of Jesus was to fulfil the will and purpose of the Father who had called him at his baptism and who had there foreshadowed his destiny of death and resurrection. Giving his life as a ransom sacrifice for many was precisely what God had sent him into the world to do. The self-giving of Jesus expressed the self-giving of God himself. In this reinterpretation a richer and more profound meaning shines through, a more explicitly God-related meaning.

The Acts of the Apostles' chapter 6 has traditionally been taken to refer to the appointment of the first deacons, the Seven, and has strongly influenced the understanding of the role of deacons in the Reformation traditions, including the sixteenth-century Church of England. However, in Acts the Seven are never called deacons as such. On the contrary, Philip and Stephen are clearly gifted evangelists: Philip brings the gospel to North Africa, through the conversion of the Ethiopian eunuch, and Stephen gains the glory of being the first Christian martyr. The traditional interpretation of the role of the Seven has been mesmerized by the word *diakonia* in 6.1, usually translated 'the distribution', i.e. of food, and the corresponding verb *diakonein* in 6.2, usually rendered 'serving at tables'. But both the immediate and the wider contexts suggest that this conventional translation of *diakon-* words in Luke 6 is in fact eccentric and not in keeping with the central meaning of the terms.

As far as the immediate context of this passage is concerned, Luke uses *diakonein* in 6.4 to refer to the ministry of the word by the Apostles and stresses that this was their first priority. This is in fact his characteristic use of the term throughout Luke–Acts. The trend is set in the first chapter of the Acts when a successor to Judas has to be found to make up the number Twelve. The special apostolic mission to witness to the risen Lord and to carry the gospel to the ends of the earth (Acts 1.8) is termed *diakonia*. Significantly *diakonia* is paralleled with the calling of the Apostles: 'this ministry and apostleship' (1.25). If we let the true sense of *diakonia* as commissioned agency have its due weight we see how closely it corresponds to apostleship. This conjunction of meanings suggests a radical alternative reading of Acts 6.

It is more than possible that in Acts 6, Luke is not concerned with the fair sharing out of food – as Collins quips, the Apostles were not running a soup kitchen – any more than he is concerned with a supposed institution of the diaconate as part of the threefold ministry. His focus is on the progress and spread of the word of God, the good news of Jesus Christ (6.7). Stephen's speech to the Sanhedrin, Philip's biblical exposition to the Ethiopian official, and the conversion of Saul – the episodes that follow – bear this out. When Paul has completed his three great missionary journeys and takes stock in his address to the Ephesian elders he sums up his apostolic ministry as 'the *diakonia* that I have received from the Lord Jesus, to testify to the good news of God's grace' (Acts 20.24). We might add to this Colossians 1.23–26 where Paul says that the ministry (*diakonia*: vv. 23, 25) that he has received in the divine economy (*oikonomia*) is that of making the word of God fully known, the mystery that has been hidden throughout the ages but has now been revealed by God to his saints, that of 'Christ in you, the hope of glory'.

Collins therefore argues on the basis of ancient Greek usage of this term and in the light of the Lukan context that the daily *diakonia* in which the widows were being neglected was not the distribution of food, but the ministry of the word. They needed to hear it in their own tongue and in their own homes.

If the meaning of *diakon-* words in these Pauline and Lukan sources is dynamic and functional, by the time we reach the Pastoral Epistles function has begun to give way to office: the deacons have become a distinct cadre of ministers, just as the *episcopoi* have. Thus several deacons minister on behalf of one *episcopos*. Linked with the male deacons are women deacons (the reference to women is sandwiched between instructions regarding deacons) who have specific but similar instructions given to them (1 Timothy 3.11). Though the *charismata* of prophecy, etc., are still present in the Pastorals, there is the beginning of a shift from the charismatic to the structural and institutional. This development is apparent not only in the Pastorals but also in the early post-apostolic writings, but it should not be exaggerated. *Diakonia* could readily become the term for an office (and later an order) in the Church because all along it carried connotations of commissioning, authority and mission.

In the *Didache* overseers (*episkopoi*) and deacons perform the eucharistic liturgy, where previously prophets and teachers had done so (15.1). In the *Shepherd of Hermas* deacons are apparently beginning to assume an administrative role (in this case, responsibility for administering charitable funds). St Ignatius of Antioch depicts the bishop as presiding in the Church in the place of God and the presbyters as standing in the place of the Apostles. The deacons are entrusted with 'the *diakonia* of Jesus Christ' (Magnesians 6.1). Just as Jesus fulfilled the will and purpose of the Father, so deacons are to carry out the instructions of the bishop as his envoy. About a century later Hippolytus portrays deacons being ordained to the service of the bishop, as in a sense his executive officers. As the bishop (and he alone) lays hands on them, he invokes the sending of Jesus Christ to do the Father's will. Throughout these sub-apostolic texts the core meaning of *diakonia* as a commission to carry out a task on behalf of one in authority persists.

I cannot emphasize too much that the case that I am putting forward does not stand or fall with Collins' thesis. It does not depend on whether his argument is accepted lock, stock and barrel. Anyone with eyes to see can see that when Paul uses *diakon-* words he is usually speaking, not of service to the community (though that is entailed and is not being challenged), but of his God-given mandate to proclaim the mystery of Christ. Any reader of the Greek New Testament can see that humble service is an inept and inappropriate hermeneutic at least for Paul's and Luke's use of these terms.

The revisionist interpretation of *diakon-* words that we owe to Collins transforms our reading of the New Testament and therefore has major implications for our understanding not only of the ministry of deacons but of all ministry, ordained and lay alike. If Collins' case is accepted – and I am not aware that it has been fundamentally challenged – the rhetoric of deacons being ordained to humble service, especially of the needy, must be dropped. Of course servanthood is not abolished. All Christian ministry – all Christian discipleship for that matter – involves humble, self-giving care of those in need. This usage of *diakonia* is certainly present even in St Paul (2 Corinthians 9.1, 12, 13: service through the collection of alms). Deacons, like all Christians, are disciples of the Suffering Servant of Second-Isaiah. But whose servant is he? Not the Servant of Israel – he is Israel (as well as the fulfilment of Israel)! He is emphatically the Servant of the Lord, of Yahweh: 'my Servant' (Isaiah 41.8; 42.1, 19; 43.10; 44.1, 21; 45.4; 49.6; 50.10; 53.11). A *diakonos* is the servant primarily of the one who sends; secondarily of those to whom he or she is sent. There is fundamental difference between service of others, where they set the agenda – a servant cannot say: I am your servant and this is what I have decided I am going to do for you – and service of God where God sets the agenda because that is God's sole prerogative. When the New Testament term *diakonia* is employed to legitimate a 'welfare' under-standing of diaconal ministry something that now appears rather dubious is going on: 'a feigned biblical authority' is being used 'for an idea that the biblical term could never express' (Collins 2002: 136).

In English 'servant' and 'minister' have rather different overtones, although the meanings overlap. For example, there is the civil servant and there is the government minister. The government minister has responsibilities placed upon him or her on behalf of the Crown and the civil servant's role is to help carry them out. Servant and minister are not convertible in this context: one could not say 'civil minister' and 'government servant', even though the minister is a servant of the Crown and the civil servant has responsibilities to administer. The choice of word makes a point. Our modern biblical translations are making a point when they choose to render *diakonos* as 'servant'; and the reconstructed theology of the diaconate and of holy order generally is making a point when it renders *diakonos* as 'minister'. The point is the connection with the ministry of Jesus Christ.

Deacons, like priests and bishops, are ordained to the ministry of Christ, a ministry that is not one of general service but is specific and distinct and can be exegeted by means of the scheme 'prophet, priest and king'. Diaconal ministry consists of the diaconal expression of the one mission and ministry – a ministry of word, sacrament and pastoral responsibility – that is entrusted to the Church. Because of this, deacons stand in a special relationship, first, to the bishop, who has oversight of all ministry among the portion of the people of God entrusted to his care; second, to the presbyters, who share that oversight in a devolved way; and, third, to the whole community of the faithful among whom the bishop presides. Deacons are sent with authority to assist the bishop and presbyters in the ministry of word and sacrament, delivered with pastoral compassion to all who need to hear the good news and to be made whole. In relation to both clergy and people they embody and model the gospel commission that gives the Church its raison d'être.

The diaconate should be understood in much more than functional terms. It is a sign of what the Church is, an ecclesial sign. It is a sign, therefore, not only to the Church but also to the world. The bridging, go-between role of deacons becomes significant here, their involvement in and linking of the divine liturgy and the needs of the unchurched out in the community. The office of deacon may be said to be also a sacramental sign because ordination is an action that has a sacramental nature in terms of the understanding of a sacrament in the Catechism in the Book of Common Prayer: it is indisputably an outward, visible sign of an inward action or grace of the Holy Spirit. The diaconate stands for the commissioned, mandated character of the whole Church as 'sign, instrument and foretaste' of the

Kingdom of God. Diaconal ministry embodies the fundamental commission of the Church in the service of the Lord. In this sense, it is representational of the commissioned, apostolic character of the whole body of the baptized. It is, so to speak, a flagship ministry with significance for all Christians.

It is on this fundamental commission that priestly and episcopal ministry (for those who are priests and bishops) rests. The new hermeneutic of *diakonia* shows why it has always been right to say, 'Once a deacon, always a deacon', and why sequential (as opposed to direct, *per saltem*) ordination makes sense. Any further ordination can only be built on the foundation of the diaconate. The reconstructed theology of the diaconate as an ecclesial sign of the fundamental divine commission of the Church to carry out the three central tasks (*tria munera*) given by Christ strongly reinforces the wisdom of the traditional practice of sequential ordination. The case for sequential ordination looks much weaker and the case for direct ordination appears correspondingly stronger where the diaconate is understood as a sign of servanthood and is not directly related to the *tria munera*. Vatican II gave a new impetus to the distinctive (or permanent) diaconate, but perhaps because the Council did not relate it very explicitly to the *tria munera*, Roman Catholic bishops' conferences around the world have sometimes struggled to implement this initiative.

One reason why, in episcopally ordered churches, bishops ordain is that they embrace within their order the other two orders. Although direct ordination to the presbyterate and even to the episcopate has not been regarded as invalid, and is not a church-dividing matter, it has been regarded as irregular since the time of St Cyprian (Wright 1993; but cf. Gibaut 2003 and Gibaut in Holeton *et al.* 1997; Wood 2000: 166–71). While there are those who advocate direct ordination to the presbyterate, mainly because they want to affirm and safeguard the distinctiveness of the diaconate,

I am not aware that direct ordination to the episcopate is being canvassed (even though there are ancient precedents). But if the episcopate builds on the presbyterate, the presbyterate in turn builds on the diaconate. *Diakonia* is the sine qua non of ordained ministry because in the ordination of deacons the divine commission that is the essence of the apostolicity of the Church is signified sacramentally.

What is given in ordination?

We are now in a better position to offer an answer to the cluster of questions that we raised at the beginning of this book: why ordain? What difference does the ordination of a member of the *laos*, of the royal, prophetic priesthood make? What do we receive in ordination that we did not have before? How does ordination change a person's identity? The answer involves five affirmations:

1. Ordination involves the public recognition of the gifts and calling that come from God and are discerned by the Church. That public recognition is reflected particularly in the examination of the candidates and the prayers. God is acknowledged as the author of ministry and as the one who ordains. We could say that an ordination serves to witness an act of God. It also expresses the consent of the Church to the choice of a minister. The rite of ordination makes the acknowledgement of gifts and calling on the part of the Church public and formal.

2. Ordination sets the public acknowledgement of God's call, God's gifts and God's authority in the context of liturgy, that is to say in the context of thanksgiving and adoration, of humble dependence and inter-cession, of the invoking of the Holy Spirit, of sacramental grace, of Christian fellowship. As an outward, visible sign of an inward, spiritual grace,

contained in the rite as well as in the candidate, ordination partakes of a sacramental quality.

3. Ordination conveys the strength for the designated task. There is prayer for spiritual grace, strength or power and the promise that the prayer will be heard. For example, the prayer that God will 'pour upon them [the candidates] the grace of his heavenly benediction'. The *Veni creator spiritus* is solemnly sung on one's knees at the ordination of priests and bishops. Both the classic formulae of ordination and the modern ones are eloquent of grace being bestowed: 'Receive the Holy Ghost ...' or 'Send down the Holy Spirit ...', etc.

4. Ordination conveys authority to minister in the Church in the name of God. 'Take thou authority ...'. We are given this authority not as something that we can wield freely but as something that is over us and to which we ourselves are subordinate. No one has the right to take the ordained ministry upon themselves. It never becomes our possession. We remain subject to the authority that is vested in our office – the authority of the Scriptures, the givenness of the sacraments and the authority of the whole people of God among whom, with whom and to whom the ordained are sent to minister pastoral care and oversight.

5. Ordination inducts the candidate into a complex new set of relationships involving both privileges and obligations. There is a new relationship to God (in the fulfilment of one's calling and in dependence on God's grace); a new relationship to the whole priestly body of the Church (one of representation and at the same time of interdependence); a new relationship to ministerial colleagues (one of collegiality and also of canonical obedience to ecclesiastical superiors) and last but by no means least important,

a new relationship to 'the world', to those 'outside' the Church, to the local community, indeed to every person one passes in the street. This last set of relationships is fraught with excessive expectations: both golden pastoral opportunities and possibilities of serious misunderstanding.

Clearly there are, in all Churches, ministries that are ordained and ministries that are not ordained but remain lay ministries. How is the distinction decided? What is the demarcation line and why is it where it is? Should it be moved so that, for example, deacons ceased to be ordained or readers and lay pastoral assistants began to be ordained? If I were asked, Should such and such a ministry be the subject of ordination?, I would offer three criteria for ordained ministry.

1. Ordained ministry is necessarily a full, triple ministry, not a partial one. It is related to word, sacrament and pastoral responsibility, the three missiological tasks (*munera*) of the Church, and not merely to one or two of them.
2. Ordained ministry involves a lifelong calling, not a temporary avocation; ordination marks one for life (the essential meaning of 'character') and is in that sense indelible. The special set of relationships that ordination creates are permanent. Ordination cannot be repeated.
3. Ordination involves a formal intention in making that ministry that it should be a ministry of the Christian Church as such, not simply a local ministry. At least in principle and in aspiration, an ordained ministry in one Church is interchangeable with an ordained ministry in another and is to that extent an instrument of communion between the Churches.

If these three criteria were applied to demarcation issues between lay and ordained ministry, we might well see some

116

movement, possibly with traffic in both directions. It might lead, for example, to the re-discernment of the vocation of a proportion of lay ministers, such as Anglican readers, and it might point to some reconsideration or refinement of the notion of local ordained ministry.

Development and reform

As I have already implied, I believe that the primary area for reform and development in the ordination services of a number of Churches (including my own, the Church of England) is that of the diaconate. This is not because I am suffering from an obsession with the diaconate, but because if – at last! – we can get the diaconate right this will help us to reach a true understanding of presbyteral and episcopal ministry as well. The reform of the diaconate is required by recent biblical interpretation (especially the work of John N. Collins), by the missionary needs of the Church in society (which demands that all forms of ministry be reconstrued in a missiological way) and by ecumenical developments and the experience of a distinctive diaconate in Anglican and other Churches (see *For Such a Time as This*, 2001).

Ordination services for the diaconate (such as the Church of England's ASB ordinal of 1980) often emphasize the servant nature of the diaconate that was prevalent until the 1990s. This now seems seriously unreconstructed and savours of the ideological. In a culture that has major problems in handling authority, the temptation is to say: We do not claim authority, we renounce all power, we are merely servants; if you don't like what we offer you, tentatively and in all humility, feel free to ignore us! It also jars when, at the ordination of deacons, bishops, who often seem to be at the top of the sacred pyramid, solemnly remind those at the bottom that they are there to serve.

The apostolic language of ambassador or envoy is highly appropriate for deacons. Their role can be seen as making connections between the eucharistic heart of the Church and pastoral needs in the community. It is not simply liturgical or simply pastoral, but involves holding the two together on behalf of the Church. The deacon, therefore, has an overriding missionary and evangelistic task. Of course this is not unique to the deacon, nor should the whole burden of the Church's evangelistic task be thrust upon the diaconate. *Diakonia* belongs to the whole body and to every Christian. Its source is our baptismal mandate in the service of Christ and his gospel. What deacons do is to represent in terms of holy order, as an ecclesial sign and in a sacramental way, what is true of the Church and to embody, reflect and release that for the benefit of all.

The Church's divine commission as herald of the gospel, which is expressed representatively and sacramentally in the ordination of deacons, underlies all ministry, ordained and lay. Therefore this understanding of *diakonia* strengthens the claim both of a distinctive diaconate and of sequential ordination, even though there is a tension between these two implications. Above all, there is an imperative, connected with the very heart of the Church's ministry, that the meaning of *diakonia* should shine out bright and clear: this can most effectively be done through a distinctive diaconate. It can be argued that it is vital, in order for the Church to be true to itself, that it should provide for a distinctive diaconate, one fulfilling the tasks I have indicated above. However, I do not think that precludes sequential ordination, through diaconate to priesthood or presbyterate. Indeed, I believe that it demands it – provided that all deacons are enabled to live into their calling for an adequate period of time, to experience and know what it is to be a deacon – and I think that that must take considerably longer than a year (some would argue for five, but three years seems about the right balance; even two would be an improvement on the current norm).

This view of *diakonia* has a knock-on effect on presbyteral and episcopal ministry. It brings out its missiological and evangelistic nature. Presbyters are missionary priests and bishops are missionary bishops – the bishop in mission is not a mode the bishop assumes from time to time, but is a permanent state of ministry (as the 1998 Lambeth Conference recognized). The bishop both engages in mission and has oversight of mission. Bishops are called 'to promote [the Church's] mission throughout the world' (as the Church of England's ASB ordinal proclaims). The role of the bishop as the chief pastor of the portion of the people of God committed to his care (cf. Canon C18 of the Church of England) has vast missiological implications. It suggests a pastoral mission throughout the diocese and its component parishes (and in the institutions of civil society through sector ministry) – a pastoral mission carried out through the sensitive and flexible ministry of word, sacrament and pastoral care to all who are willing to receive it.

In this respect we can see clearly how diaconal ministry ties in with the ministry of the priest and the bishop. Deacons have a whole ministry, not simply a pastoral ministry. It is one of word and sacrament, as well as of pastoral care (but assisting and not presiding). That ministry in its wholeness is the form taken by the mission of the Church, its set of core tasks. The Church's part in God's mission takes the form of a ministry carried out through preaching and teaching, the celebration and administration of the sacraments and pastoral responsibility – that is to say, through the threefold mandate of word, sacrament and pastoral care, as suggested by the Great Commission of Matthew 28 which speaks of making disciples, baptizing and teaching. The most far-reaching reform or development in our understanding of ordination that I believe is called for today is to shape ministry, ordained and lay, to the demands of mission. After all, in the Church the mission of God takes the form of a ministry. The renewal of the diaconate could blaze a trail for the transformation of presbyteral and episcopal ministry also into a missiological mode, while lighting a beacon for all the royal priesthood. The ministries of the Church are full and equal because they are ministries of Christ. Each order, as an ecclesial sign, proclaims something of the nature of his body and points to the mission of God that calls the Church into being and gives it its purpose.

REFERENCES

Abbott, W. M., ed., 1966. *The Documents of Vatican II*, London: Geoffrey Chapman.

Abraham, W., 1989. *The Logic of Evangelism*, London: Hodder & Stoughton and Grand Rapids, Mich.: Eerdmans.

[ACC] Anglican Consultative Council, 1990. *Mission in a Broken World*, London: Church House Publishing.

Althaus, P., 1966. *The Theology of Martin Luther*, Philadelphia, Pa.: Fortress Press.

Anglican–Methodist Covenant, 2001. London: Church House Publishing; Peterborough: Methodist Publishing House.

Anglican–Methodist International Commission, 1996. *Sharing in the Apostolic Communion*, Lake Junaluska, NC: World Methodist Council.

Aquinas, T., *Summa Theologiae*, n.d.. London: Eyre & Spottiswoode and New York: McGraw-Hill (Blackfriars edn), vol. 16.

[ARCIC] Anglican–Roman Catholic International Commission, 1982. *The Final Report*, London: CTS and SPCK.

Augustine, 1972. *The City of God*, trans H. Bettenson, Harmondsworth: Penguin.

Avis, P., 1981. *The Church in the Theology of the Reformers*, London: Marshall, Morgan & Scott; (reprinted Wipf and Stock, 2002).

— 1989. *Eros and the Sacred*, London: SPCK.

— 1990. *Christians in Communion*, London: Geoffrey Chapman Mowbray.

— 1999a. *Anglican Orders and the Priesting of Women*, London: Darton, Longman & Todd.

— 1999b. *God and the Creative Imagination: Metaphor, Symbol and Myth in Religion and Theology*, London and New York: Routledge.

— 2000. *The Anglican Understanding of the Church: An Introduction*, London: SPCK.

— 2001. *Church, State and Establishment*, London: SPCK.

— 2002. *Anglicanism and the Christian Church*, revised and expanded edn, London: T&T Clark/Continuum.

— 2003. *A Church Drawing Near: Spirituality and Mission in a Post-Christian Culture*, London: T&T Clark International.

Avis, P., ed., 2002. *The Christian Church: An Introduction to the Major Traditions*, London: SPCK.

— ed., 2003a. *Public Faith? The State of Religious Belief and Practice in Britain*, London: SPCK.

— ed., 2003b. *Seeking the Truth of Change in the Church: Reception, Communion and the Ordination of Women*, London: T&T Clark International.

Barrett, C. K., 1962. *The Epistle to the Romans* (Black's New Testament Commentaries), London: A. & C. Black.

— 1973. *The Second Epistle to the Corinthians* (Black's New Testament Commentaries), London: A. & C. Black.

— 1985. *Church, Ministry and Sacraments in the New Testament*, Exeter: Paternoster.

Bell, G. K. A., 1954. *The Kingship of Christ*: Harmondsworth: Penguin.

Best, E., 1981. *Following Jesus: Discipleship in the Gospel of Mark*, Sheffield: JSNT Supplementary Series, 4.

[BEM], 1982. *Baptism, Eucharist and Ministry*, Geneva: WCC.

[BMU] Board of Mission and Unity], 1987. *The Measure of Mission*, London: BMU and PWM.

Bonhoeffer, D., 1959. *The Cost of Discipleship*, London: SCM Press.

Bosch, D. J., 1991. *Transforming Mission*, Maryknoll, NY: Orbis.

Bouteneff, P. C. and Falconer, A. D., eds, 1999. Episkopé *and Episcopacy and the Quest for Visible Unity: Two Consultations*, Geneva: WCC.

'Called to Common Mission', An Agreement between the Episcopal Church in the USA and the Evangelical Lutheran Church in America, 1999.

Called to Love and Praise, 1999. Peterborough: Methodist Publishing House.

Calvin, J., 1961. *The Epistles of Paul the Apostle to the Romans and to the Thessalonians* (Calvin's Commentaries), Edinburgh: The Saint Andrew Press.

— 1962. *Institutes of the Christian Religion*, trans. Henry Beveridge, 2 vols, London: James Clarke.

Carey, G., 1997. 'The Way Ahead: Preparing the Church of England for the New Millennium' (The Ashe Lecture), Private Circulation.

Carr, W., 1985. *The Priestlike Task*, London: SPCK.

Church Assembly, 1945. *Towards the Conversion of England: A Report of a Commission on Evangelism Appointed by the Archbishops of Canterbury and York*, Westminster: Church Assembly.

Clark, N., 1992. *Pastoral Care in Context*, Bury St Edmunds: Kevin Mayhew.

Cocksworth, C., 1993. *Evangelical Eucharistic Thought in the Church of England*, Cambridge: Cambridge University Press.

Cocksworth, C. and Brown, R., 2002. *Being a Priest Today*, Norwich: Canterbury Press.

Coleridge, S. T., 1884. *Table Talk*, Morley, H., ed., London: Routledge.

Collins, J. N., 1990. *Diakonia: Re-interpreting the Ancient Sources*, Oxford: Oxford University Press.

— 1992. *Are All Christians Ministers?*, Newtown, NSW/ Brunswick, Victoria: E.J. Dwyer/David Lovell.

— 2002. *Deacons and the Church: Making Connections Between Old and New*, Leominster: Gracewing.

Commitment to Mission and Unity, 1996. London: Church House Publishing and Peterborough: Methodist Publishing House.

Congar, Y. M. J., 1959. *Lay People in the Church*, London: Geoffrey Chapman.

Croft, S., 1999. *Ministry in Three Dimensions*, London: Darton, Longman & Todd.

Dewar, F., 1991. *Called or Collared? An Alternative Approach to Vocation*, London: SPCK.

Doctrine Commission, 1938. *Doctrine in the Church of England: The Report of the Commission on Christian Doctrine appointed by the Archbishops of Canterbury and York in 1922*, London: SPCK.

Dudley, M., 1983. 'Is Ordination a Sacrament?', *Heythrop Journal*, 24: 149–58.

Dugmore, C. W., 1958. *The Mass and the English Reformers*, London: Macmillan.

Evans, G. R., ed., 2000. *A History of Pastoral Care*, London and New York: Cassell.

Flannery, A., ed., 1982. *Vatican Council II: More Post Conciliar Documents*, New York: Costello.

For Such a Time as This: A Renewed Diaconate in the Church of England, 2001. London: Church House Publishing.

Ford, D. F., 1999. *Self and Salvation: Being Transformed*, Cambridge: Cambridge University Press.

Gibaut, J. St.-H., 2003. *Sequential or Direct Ordination?* Cambridge: Grove Books.

Goergen, D. J. and Garrido, A., eds, 2000. *The Theology of Priesthood*, Collegeville, Minn.: Liturgical Press.

Gore, C., 1889. *The Church and the Ministry*, 2nd edn, London: Longmans & Co [title page: *The Ministry of the Christian Church*; Rivingtons].

Grabbe, L. L., 1995. *Priests, Prophets, Diviners, Sages: A Socio-Historical Study of Religious Specialists in Ancient Israel*, Valley Forge, Pa.: Trinity Press International.

Graham, E., 1996. *Transforming Practice: Pastoral Theology in an Age of Uncertainty*, London: Mowbray.

Grainger, R., 1988. *The Message of the Rite: The Significance of Christian Rites of Passage*, Cambridge: Lutterworth.

Green, Michael, 1970. *Evangelism in the New Testament*, London: Hodder & Stoughton.

Greenwood, R., 1994. *Transforming Priesthood*, London: SPCK.

Gros, J., Meyer, H. and Rusch, W., eds, 2000. *Growth in Agreement II*, Geneva: WCC and Grand Rapids, Mich.: Eerdmans.

GROU, 1984. *God's Reign and Our Unity: Report of the International Anglican–Reformed Dialogue.* Edinburgh: St Andrew Press and London: SPCK.

Gundry, R. H., 1994. *Matthew: A Commentary on His Handbook for a Mixed Church under Persecution*, Grand Rapids, Mich.: Eerdmans.

Hall, C. and Hannaford, R., eds, 1996. *Order and Ministry*, Leominster: Gracewing.

Hanson, A. T., 1961. *The Pioneer Ministry*, London: SCM Press.

Hannaford, R., 1991. 'Towards a Theology of the Diaconate', in C. Hall, ed., *The Deacon's Ministry*, Leominster: Gracewing.

Hardy, D. W. and Ford, D. F., 1984. *Jubilate: Theology in Praise*, London: Darton, Longman & Todd.

Hefling, C., 2003. 'What Do We Bless and Why?', *Anglican Theological Review*, 85(1): 87–96.

Holeton, D., *et al.*, 1997. *Anglican Orders and Ordinations* (International Anglican Liturgical Consultation, 1997), Cambridge: Grove Books.

Hollenbach, D., 2002. *The Common Good and Christian Ethics*, Cambridge: Cambridge University Press.

Hoskyns, E. and Davey, N., 1947. *The Fourth Gospel*, 2nd edn, London: Faber.

Houlden, J. L., 2002. 'Why Were the Disciples Ever Called Disciples?', *Theology*, 105: 411–17.

House of Bishops, 1997. *Eucharistic Presidency*, London: Church House Publishing.

— 2000. *Bishops in Communion*: An Occasional Paper of the House of Bishops of the Church of England, London: Church House Publishing.

John Paul II, 2003. *Pastores gregis* (Post-Synodal Apostolic Exhortation on the Bishop), www.vatican.va.

Johnson, M., ed., 1990. *Thomas Cranmer: Essays*, Durham: Turnstone Ventures.

Kruse, C., 1983. *New Testament Foundations of Ministry*, Basingstoke: Marshall, Morgan and Scott.

Käsemann, E., 1964. 'Ministry and Community in the New Testament', in *Essays on New Testament Themes*, London: SCM Press.

Küng, H., 1972. *Why Priests?*, London: Collins/Fontana.

Le Grys, A., 1998. *Preaching to the Nations: The Origins of Mission in the Early Church*, London: SPCK.

Legood, G., ed., 1999. *Chaplaincy: The Church's Sector Ministries*, London: Cassell.

Lightfoot, J. B., 1898. 'Dissertation: The Christian Ministry' in *St Paul's Epistle to the Philippians*, 12th edn, London: Macmillan.

— 1905. *St Paul's Epistle to the Galatians*, London: Macmillan.

MacIntyre, A., 1985. *After Virtue*, 2nd edn, London: Duckworth.

McNeill, J. T., 1952. *A History of the Cure of Souls*, London: SCM Press (New York: Harper Brothers, 1951).

Marriage, A., 1995. *The People of God: A Royal Priesthood*, London: Darton, Longman & Todd.

Maurice, F. D., 1958. *The Kingdom of Christ*, 2 vols, A. Vidler, ed., London: SCM Press.

[Meissen], 1992. *The Meissen Agreement: Texts*, London: Council for Christian Unity.

Miller, C., 2002. 'The Theology of the Laity: Description and Construction with Reference to the American Book of Common Prayer', *Anglican Theological Review*, 84: 219–38.

Moberly, R. C., 1969. *Ministerial Priesthood*, 2nd edn with an introduction by A. T. Hanson, London: SPCK.

Moltmann, J., 1977. *The Church in the Power of the Spirit*, London: SCM Press.

Newman, J. H., 1990. *The Via Media of the Anglican Church*, ed. and introduced H. D. Weidner, Oxford: Clarendon Press.

Niagara, 1988. *The Niagara Report of the Anglican–Lutheran Consultation on Episcope 1987*, London: Church House Publishing.

O'Meara, T. F., 1983. *Theology of Ministry*, New York: Paulist Press.

Office of Bishop, 1993. Geneva: Lutheran World Federation.

Osborne, K., 1988. *Priesthood*, New York: Paulist Press.

— 1993. *Ministry: Lay Ministry in the Roman Catholic Church: Its History and Theology*, New York/Mahwah: Paulist Press.

Pattison, S., 1988. *A Critique of Pastoral Care*, London: SCM Press.

[Porvoo], 1993. *Together in Mission and Ministry: The Porvoo Common Statement*, London: Church House Publishing.

Power, D. N., 1969. *Ministers of Christ and his Church*, London: Geoffrey Chapman.

— 1992. 'Representing Christ in Community and Sacrament' in Goergen, D., ed., *Being a Priest Today*, Collegeville: Liturgical Press, pp. 97–123.

[Pullach], 1973. *Anglican–Lutheran International Conversations (1970–72): The Pullach Report*, London: SPCK.

Raiser, K., 1999. ' "That the World May Believe": The missionary vocation as the necessary horizon for ecumenism', *International Review of Mission*, 88: 187–96.

Reid, J. K. S., 1955. *The Biblical Doctrine of the Ministry*, Edinburgh: Oliver and Boyd (Scottish Journal of Theology Occasional Papers, 4).

Richardson, A., 1958. *An Introduction to the Theology of the New Testament*, London: SCM Press.

Ritchie, J. M., 1967. 'The Missionary Significance of the Sacraments', *Scottish Journal of Theology* 20: 37–49.

Robinson, J. A. T., 1953. 'The One Baptism as a Category of New Testament Soteriology', *Scottish Journal of Theology*, 6: 257–74 (also in *Twelve New Testament Studies*, London: SCM, 1962).

Samuel, V. and Sugden, C., eds, 1999. *Mission as Transformation*, Oxford: Regnum Books.

Schweizer, E., 1961. *Church Order in the New Testament*, London: SCM Press.

Sykes, S. W., 1995. *Unashamed Anglicanism*, London: Darton, Longman & Todd.

Sykes, S. W., ed., 1991. *Sacrifice and Redemption: Durham Essays in Theology*, Cambridge: Cambridge University Press.

Sykes, S. W., Booty, J. and Knight, J., eds, 1998. *The Study of Anglicanism*, 2nd edn, London: SPCK and Philadelphia, Pa.: Fortress Press.

Tappert, T. G., ed., 1959. *The Book of Concord*, Philadelphia, Pa.: Fortress Press.

The World Mission of the Church: Tambaran, 1938. London and New York: International Missionary Council.

Thiselton, A., 2000. *The First Epistle to the Corinthians* (NIGTC), Grand Rapids, Mich.: Eerdmans and Carlisle: Paternoster.

Torrance, T. F., 1955. *Royal Priesthood*, Edinburgh: Oliver and Boyd (*Scottish Journal of Theology* Occasional Papers, 3).

— 1959. *Conflict and Agreement in the Church*, 2 vols, London: Lutterworth Press.

— 1966. 'The Mission of the Church', *Scottish Journal of Theology* 19: 129–43.

Wainwright, G., 1997. *For Our Salvation: Two Approaches to the Work of Christ*, London: SPCK and Grand Rapids, Mass.: Eerdmans.

Weil, L., 2002. *A Theology of Worship*, Cambridge, MA: Cowley Publications.

Williams, R., 1999. 'Being a People: Reflections on the Concept of Laity', *Religion, State and Society*, 27: 11–21.

Wingren, G., 1964. *Gospel and Church*, Edinburgh and London: Oliver and Boyd.

Wood, S. K., 2000. *Sacramental Orders*, Collegeville, Minn.: Liturgical Press.

— ed., 2003. *Ordering the Baptismal Priesthood: Theologies of Lay and Ordained Ministry*, Collegeville, Minn.: Liturgical Press.

Wright, J. R., 1993. 'Sequential or Cumulative Orders vs. Direct Ordination', *Anglican Theological Review*, 75: 246–51.

Zizioulas, J. D., 1985. *Being as Communion*, New York: St Vladimir's Seminary Press.

NAME INDEX

Problem: 3-fold definition of ministry
based on Mt 28, especially "making disciples"
as the term that substantiates "pastoral
responsibility." (23-24, 49) See 81! 96, 101

KoG 57, 68, 94

Demands of mission call for 'personal ministry' —
episkope! 86
Definition of Mission 93ff.

What is meant by authority? p. 99, 115

Rejection of the humility of diakonia! 110
missional meaning of diakonia — 117

Check our critical response to Collins'
work.

Strengths

- Missional definition of ministry
    Missio Dei!
- Ecumenical appreciation although
    predominantly Anglican
- Lucid, clear, accessible